PRINCE
HARRY

PRINCE HARRY

THE BIOGRAPHY

MARK SAUNDERS

JOHN BLAKE

Published by John Blake Publishing Ltd, 3 Bramber Court,
2 Bramber Road, London W14 9PB, England

First published in hardback in 2002

ISBN 1 904034 18 7

British Library Cataloguing-in-Publication Data: A catalogue record
for this book is available from the British Library.

Design by ENVY

Printed and bound in Great Britain by CPD (Wales)

1 3 5 7 9 10 8 6 4 2

Papers used by John Blake Publishing Ltd are natural, recyclable products
made from wood grown in sustainable forests. The manufacturing processes
conform to the environmental regulations of the country of origin

For Martin and Jasmine

CONTENTS

ACKNOWLEDGEMENTS

Many thanks to: John Matthews, Keith Badman,
Kelvin Bruce, Trevor Adams, Stuart Clements,
Don Sargeant, Joan Blanchfield and Carmen Vana.

I would also like to thank my publisher John Blake
and, of course, far too much love to my old friend,
partner and sounding board Glenn Harvey.

INTRODUCTION

ON A SUN-KISSED Saturday afternoon in June 1995, Ludgrove School held its annual sports day. The event, attended by parents and friends of the school's pupils, is the highlight of the summer calendar at Ludgrove, held just before the pupils break up for their summer holiday. This was one of the years when the occasion was further enhanced by the school's most famous boarders, Princes William and Harry, who, as always, had been joined at the school by their estranged parents, the Prince and Princess of Wales.

As Charles and Diana walked among the picnicking families, their tartan blankets laid out behind the obligatory Range Rovers, they occasionally stopped to chat with some of the other parents. Diana, in particular, loved to gossip with the mums and their children, catching up with tales that invariably involved her own two children.

Charles and Diana, by all appearances, were the perfect couple that long ago Saturday afternoon. They knew the world's fascination with the break-up of their marriage continued unabated, and were determined that the mass ranks of press photographers, lined up in bushes some half a mile away, would not be getting any pictures to prolong the story. Still, the Nikon chorus sprung into action as Charles and Diana made their way across the sprawling fields of Ludgrove School towards the running track where Prince William was due to take part in the hundred yards race.

At the same time, their youngest son Prince Harry and three of his friends were preparing a show that would make the hundred yards sprint, in common with every other event that day, cease to matter. As the assorted parents and friends made their way towards the track, Harry and his mates climbed up on to a wooden fence and, in full view of all the spectators, pulled down their shorts and bared their bottoms.

Diana, aware of a commotion happening somewhere behind her, was surprised when a member of the Royal Protection Squad came across a few minutes later and spoke into her husband's ear. After a brief moment Charles, his face a picture of concern, turned to his wife and, tactfully trying to find the right words, said, 'I think Harry's got into a spot of bother ...'

'Oh Lord! What's he done now.'

CHAPTER ONE

Prince Harry could aptly be described as something of a 'war baby'. Though 15 September 1984 was long after the Falklands conflict had disappeared from the headlines, Harry was born just as another battle was taking shape. This bitter siege was waged in private and remained secret for many years afterwards, but Harry's arrival could not have been at a more tumultuous time, coming as it did at the start of the 'War of the Waleses'.

His parents' marriage was considered nothing less than rock solid back in those days. Charles and Diana were the world's darlings, two young people desperately in love and building a family. As Harry's birth approached, it seemed that on their shoulders Charles and Diana also carried the dreams and aspirations of a public that, in the early years, so desperately wanted the fairytale element of the blushing and beautiful princess and her devoted husband to be real. But the world now knows of a different story behind the fake smiles and public delight of another Crown prince.

Harry was born earlier than expected. Princess Diana began experiencing labour pains early on the Saturday morning of what was to be a quiet weekend at Windsor Castle. During the pregnancy Diana had suffered badly from morning sickness, despite maintaining a full public schedule. She had frequently complained to members of the public about suffering from this but, rather than gaining her the sympathy she was so obviously looking for, Diana's nausea merely became a topic that endeared her to the public and further enhanced her image in their eyes. The population of Britain, it seemed, really did believe the royal family had blue blood and therefore would never suffer from something as mundane as morning sickness in a serious way. Because of this it never seems to have crossed anybody's mind that a young woman on the verge of giving birth should possibly not be carrying out exhaustive royal duties. Despite the fact she was heavily pregnant, Diana had found it hard to refuse the public's demands to see their favourite princess, and carried on working despite medical advice to take things a little easier. Throughout her life Diana was to have an almost pathological fear of letting people down and it was the same during her pregnancy. Even Prince Charles, in a moment of concern, suggested she take things a little easier. It was the Queen who eventually took matters into her own hands and virtually ordered Diana to get over her innocent, and strangely touching, concerns about 'letting other people down' and rest up a bit. The Queen's concern was quite genuine. She herself had suffered badly with morning sickness prior to Prince Edward's birth. Turning to a royal aide in the eighth month of her pregnancy, Her Majesty unexpectedly blurted out, 'Good Lord, I feel absolutely wretched!'

Diana had been brought to Windsor Castle by Prince Charles, who, with the full support of the Queen and Duke of Edinburgh, considered the peace and tranquillity of the Queen's favourite home to be the perfect place for the exhausted princess to get some much needed rest. Charles also had his eye on playing polo at nearby Smiths Lawn the following day, and had not seen any reason for the imminent birth of his second son to disrupt his plans.

The castle, probably the best loved of all the royal homes, sits proudly overlooking the River Thames and takes its name from the town it dominates. Standing in 13 acres, and containing more than 1,000 rooms, Windsor Castle is the oldest royal residence, having been in continuous use since William the Conqueror chose the site for a fortress in 1066. It was a strangely appropriate place for Diana to be that Saturday, the drab grey walls and wrought iron gates reflecting her current emotional state: surrounded by the royal family yet totally alone.

By 1984, 22 years into her reign, the castle had become the Queen's favourite home, and she spent most weekends there; enjoying the tranquillity of the perfectly manicured lawns, the glorious views of Windsor Great Park and membership at one of the first video shops to open in nearby Slough. But, despite these obvious attractions, Diana entertained herself alone, watching TV and listening to her personal stereo. She also spent hours on the phone to her friends in London who cheered her up with giggly conversations about the new wardrobe Diana would need after the birth.

Charles's polo plans were nearly dashed early on Saturday morning when Diana's labour pains began. She was immediately taken to London's St Mary's Hospital, where she arrived with her husband at 7.30am. An element of farce was added to the hospital trip when one of the police cars escorting the royal couple's Ford Granada was challenged to a race by a young man in a Capri. Charles, holding Diana's hand in the back of the car, jokingly mentioned to his wife it looked like Bodie and Doyle had joined the Royal Protection Squad.

A room had already been prepared for Diana in the Hospital's Lindo Wing and it was here she was taken, with Prince Charles in attendance, to be examined by her gynaecologist, Dr George Pinker. Dr Pinker, a methodical yet friendly man, had also delivered Prince William some two years earlier. Diana was pleased he was taking care of Harry's birth too, telling Prince Charles her gynaecologist was one of the few men who could make her completely relaxed.

Harry was born at 4.20pm that afternoon, some three hours after Diana's contractions had begun to increase in number. It was not a perfect birth, and at one point Diana was given the pain-killing epidermal injection, a controversial drug that was not as routinely administered then as it is today. Throughout the ordeal Diana had sucked on an ice cube. Prince Charles was by her side, constantly mopping her brow and endlessly repeating words of encouragement. It all seemed a long way from the early stages of the labour, when Diana had actually managed to read a paperback novel whilst her husband dozed in an armchair beside the bed.

Then Harry arrived. He weighed in at 6 pounds 14 ounces, and had light blue eyes and a bit of reddish hair. Diana had always known Harry would be a boy since her child's sex had been revealed during an ultra-scan. Charles's immediate response was to make a nervous remark about the baby being a boy and having brown hair. Harry broke an amazing 36-year sequence of boy-girl royal births. Prior to him every senior royal had had a son followed by a daughter since Prince Charles was born in 1948. After Princess Anne's birth two years later, the trend was followed by Princess Margaret, the Duchess of Gloucester, the Duchess of Kent, Princess Michael of Kent, Princess Alexandra and Princess Anne.

Still, despite the wonderful support Charles had just provided, his remarks on the birth of his second son, intended, he said, to make his wife laugh after the ordeal, were misplaced. After nine hours of labour, a simple 'well done' would have sufficed. For Diana the words would have contained even more poignancy due to the fact that her own father had hoped she, the third daughter, would be a boy. Despite his royal status as substitute to Prince William, Diana vowed her son would never be treated as a second. She had already been on a shopping spree at Harrods for new clothes and toys for the baby, despite Prince Charles's protestations it was a waste of money, as William's hand-me-downs would do.

Princess Diana shook her head sadly and wondered if her husband would ever understand motherhood.

Charles immediately called the Queen at Balmoral, on a specially installed phone at Diana's bedside, to tell her that everything was OK and she had another grandson. Her Majesty, who estate workers described as 'absolutely delighted', enquired after Diana, before setting off in search of the Duke of Edinburgh to spread the good news. Prince Charles then proceeded to call the polo powers that be to say he would now definitely be playing tomorrow, before driving back to Kensington Palace to inform the two-year-old Prince William he had a new baby brother. At KP, Charles slumped, exhausted, into a chair and ordered a stiff scotch, commenting to his valet he never knew there were so many people waiting to hear the great news of the birth of his second child.

Both Charles and Diana were determined that their older son should not feel left out by the arrival of the second boy even though, due to the very nature of his birth, Harry would always play second fiddle to William. During her pregnancy, Diana had encouraged William to bond with his new brother by gently touching her tummy. (The whole bonding process was faultless: William was later to describe Harry as 'the most beautiful thing I have ever seen'.)

It was, therefore, an excited Prince William who arrived at the hospital at 9.02am the following day in a Mercedes people-carrier, accompanied by his father. Carefully tucking his shirt into his shorts as he jumped from the vehicle, William was somewhat bemused by the vast hordes of press photographers and members of the public that had begun arriving as early as dawn on that bright, crisp Sunday morning, and eagerly grinned at the cameras for the first time. Nostalgic paparazzi photographers still remember the moment with fondness. William was still too young to bear them the sort of malice that was to follow in later years.

Once inside the hospital William could contain his excitement no more and he raced down the corridor towards his mother's room after his father had said to him, 'Go on ... Mummy's down there.' Charles held back, allowing his son to run on ahead. William, aged just two-and-a-half, halted abruptly outside the room with the natural hesitancy of a child, and it wasn't until Diana herself put her head around the door that he squealed with delight and jumped into her arms. William saw his new baby brother for the first time through the strands of his mother's hair. What followed was the unique happiness known to any family that has experienced the joy of another child. It was the happiest of occasions. Diana breastfed the baby while William looked on in awe. His father, finding William's joy and natural curiosity infectious, instructed his elder son to go outside the room and tell his nanny, Nanny Barnes, to come in. On first sight of Harry, still in his mother's arms, Nanny Barnes could only exclaim, 'He's gorgeous ...'

Peals of laughter were heard coming from the room as Harry, still fast asleep, had his hand held nervously by William. Eventually, as Diana began to tire and Harry continued to sleep, Nanny Barnes took William back to Kensington Palace. Outside the hospital, Prince William could not stop talking to his nanny about Harry. But once back at

KP the excitement became too much and he immediately fell fast asleep.

Alone in the £150-a-night private room both Diana and Charles could hear the crowds outside as William left, and speculation began as to how soon it would be before Diana herself left the hospital. Had Harry been awake, or even reached consciousness, he would have heard the first of many rows that would be a feature of both his and William's young life. Charles still wanted to play polo that afternoon, and Diana begged him not to. It is difficult not to sympathise with Princess Diana, as she had virtually planned her first pregnancy around Charles's polo diary. In later years she told Andrew Morton, author of the best-selling *Diana: Her True Story*: 'When we had William we had to find a date that suited him (Charles) and his polo.'

Diana, who later claimed she knew Charles had gone back to his mistress Camilla Parker Bowles, couldn't stand the thought of the polo crowd giving Charles a hearty 'well done old chap' whilst covering up the very relationship she believed was destroying the marriage. Her resentment of her husband's polo plans in the immediate aftermath of giving birth eventually led to her realising the marriage was all but over. 'Suddenly, as Harry was born, it just went bang,' she said in later years, 'our marriage, the whole thing went down the drain.' Neither side was prepared to give, and so at 2.32pm, 22 hours and 12 minutes after giving birth, and 10 minutes after pleading with Charles not to leave her alone, Diana left the hospital with a husband who had every intention of getting his own way.

And yet it could all have been so different. Diana herself admitted that the six weeks prior to Harry's birth were the closest she and Charles had ever had, and the child was conceived by two people deeply in love – and lust. During the frantic bouts of love-making that produced Harry, both Charles and Diana discovered a fondness for sex neither had experienced before. On one memorable occasion Diana even managed to set off a full alert when her long legs tripped an alarm next to the bed during a particularly energetic session. Both Charles and Diana were equally astonished when two gun-toting police officers crashed through the door, rudely interrupting them and causing a furious reaction from Charles who demanded to know why they were there whilst trying to cover himself and his equally naked wife with the bed sheets.

Unfortunately marital bliss was not to be. The infamous 'third person' in Diana's marriage had come back on the scene prior to Harry's birth. That Charles and Camilla Parker Bowles could begin and continue a love affair behind the back of a heavily pregnant Diana is astonishing in its arrogance. Their belief that they could carry on and not be found out is almost laughable.

Via the network of gossip that is a major feature of life behind the palace walls, it had already reached Diana that Charles's affections did not lie exclusively with her, something Diana had suspected since halfway through her pregnancy, when she realised she was sleeping with a husband whose sexual desires were elsewhere. Diana herself referred to the conception as 'a miracle'. Following Charles's remarks on first seeing his second child, the penny finally dropped for

the naive former kindergarten teacher, who was to describe the moment in later years with tremendous sadness: 'Something inside me closed off. By then I knew he had gone back to his lady.'

A fanfare of bagpipes and cheers greeted the Queen as she made her first public appearance following the royal birth. The announcement of Harry's birth had come from an official bulletin promptly posted at the gates of Balmoral that read: 'Her Royal Highness The Princess Of Wales was safely delivered of a son at 4.20pm today. Her Royal Highness and the child are both well.'

Hundreds of cheering, flag-waving well-wishers lined the streets as she left Balmoral to attend church at nearby Crathie. She was joined on the half-mile trip by the Duke of Edinburgh, the Queen Mother and, ever in tow, Prince Edward, who had earlier stood up to his father during a row about his impending military career that was to be spent in the Royal Marines. Edward had decided that the morning of Harry's birth would be a good time to broach the subject of possibly not taking up the commission he had been offered. (He eventually left the Royal Marines in disgrace after only 90 days; it turned out to be one of his more successful careers.)

Two pipers and a 30-man company of Argyll and Sutherland Highlanders led the royal procession. Inside the tiny church prayers were offered and psalms sung for the new baby. The Queen was secretly delighted by the timing of the birth. The baby had originally been expected around 26 September, when she and the Duke would have been in

Canada. Grinning from ear to ear and sporting a jaunty feather cockade in her hat, the Queen beamed with pride as she waved to onlookers. Unfortunately some of Her Majesty's smiles hid a painful row she had had with her husband earlier that day when the Duke, who seemed to be rowing with everyone that weekend, had insisted he saw no reason to rush down to London to see the newborn baby. When the Queen asked, rather sarcastically by all accounts, how long it would be before he went, the Duke replied, 'I'll go when I'm ready ...' It took six weeks for the Duke to be ready to see his new grandson.

Prior to leaving St Mary's Hospital, Diana thanked all the staff personally. She then had her hair and make-up done in preparation for the 50 or so photographers who were waiting outside. No matter what the situation, Diana very rarely let the photographers down. Despite the rows with her husband and the fact she had given birth only a day earlier, Diana greeted her public – an astonishing 1,500 people had by now gathered outside the hospital – looking fresh and stunning in a smart red suit with a red-and-white striped blouse, fashionably tied at the neckline, and cradling Harry in her arms. Charles told a friendly press corps his son was 'absolutely marvellous' and, his mind still occupied with polo, added, 'We have nearly got a full polo team now.'

Excited Fleet Street reporters filed the story, silently thanking Charles for such good copy. In those days they had no idea how much Diana loathed the sport of polo. Diana's hatred of the sport had been further enhanced earlier that year when, on her 23rd birthday, she had attended a polo match near the family home of Highgrove. Tragedy struck when a young woman attempting to approach the royal box to greet Diana was knocked down and killed by a galloping horse. Diana, heavily pregnant, was deeply shaken by the incident. Prince Charles was so concerned by his wife's sadness he called in the royal doctor.

There was more sadness in the run-up to Harry's birth for Diana. In August she went as usual with Charles and William to Balmoral Castle. Charles had already promised Diana the trip would be spent together and that he had no intention of taking advantage of Balmoral's excellent shooting and gaming facilities. But on the second day of the holiday the seclusion was marred by the sad news that Diana's favourite uncle, Lord Fermoy, had committed suicide, on the grounds of his sprawling manor near the royal estate at Sandringham. Sobbing her heart out, Diana attended the funeral on her own, wearing a black maternity dress. Prince Charles had offered to go with her, but Diana, aware her husband was inundated with royal duties despite the imminent arrival of his second son, insisted she go alone, explaining to Charles he could play the doting husband after the birth. Diana wasn't being facetious, she knew Prince Charles's presence alongside her at the private funeral would attract hordes of press photographers that she had no great desire to encounter. Only three years into her public life, Diana was already starting to loathe the ever-present photographers. At the time she had no idea how much worse it was to get.

Outside the hospital, London's Town Crier, Julian Shepherd, clad in traditional red uniform that added that vital element of farce that British pomp always needs, ceremoniously rang a bell and heralded the arrival of another son for the Prince and Princess of Wales. Just across the way in Hyde Park, the Queens Troop, the Royal Horse Artillery fired a forty-one gun salute.

Unfortunately for the waiting crowds, Harry was covered in a white shawl and both press and public were disappointed to catch only a glimpse of hair and the tip of his nose. Confused tabloid readers held their newspapers upside down the following day trying to work out what the newborn baby looked like. But the lack of pictures showing Harry's face in the newspapers, and the somewhat anti-climactic television pictures that also showed nothing of Harry, failed to prevent his birth from being the biggest news story in the world. In the United States little Harry even managed to upstage the legendary Miss America beauty pageant. News of the birth broke just hours before the contest in Atlantic City, New Jersey, and the eventual winner, Miss Utah, Shariene Wells, found herself relegated to second place in newspapers and on TV beneath banner headlines proclaiming the royal birth. History relates little else of Miss Shariene Wells.

Harry's birth was the last time the British public felt obliged to celebrate at the behest of the royal family. In later years royal births and marriages were treated as part of the soap opera the House of Windsor was to become, but in 1984 people still stood for the national anthem and in the countryside they still doffed their caps to the landed gentry (it seems somewhat absurd now that anyone would even consider bowing to Prince Edward), and the news of another child for the Prince and Princess of Wales was greeted with genuine warmth.

At London's premier airport, Heathrow, special sticks of rock and postcards marking the royal birth were given away to delighted passengers preparing to board flights. The gifts each bore a cartoon of a smiling Concorde with a baby's cot hanging from its nose. They were distributed minutes after a public announcement in several different languages informed the world of Harry's birth.

Elsewhere in the country, the British reacted as only a nation that unashamedly puts Great in front of its name can. Discovering a nostalgia it had forgotten, middle England acted with enthusiasm. The ladies of the WI baked cakes, village sub-postmasters hung out the bunting and locals in pubs throughout the land toasted the newborn baby with specially brewed beer and overpriced cocktails. It was almost as if a collective sigh of relief met the announcement that Charles and Diana had now produced both an heir and a spare in just under 28 months and the bloodline of the House of Windsor was safe.

Harry, like his brother before him, was immediately bombarded with presents. Flowers, balloons, telegrams and cuddly toys began to arrive from all over the world. The American singer Barry Manilow sent a miniature antique piano, and Michael Jackson sent a stuffed monkey with a congratulatory card. His birth also triggered an explosion of souvenirs commemorating the event. China mugs, thimbles, china dolls, tea towels and any number of picture postcards instantly created a massive industry that was said to be worth

£30 million. At one point, unscrupulous dealers in America even tried to sell the sheets from Princess Diana's bed at Paddington Hospital. If the story is true, the sales would have diminished somewhat after the hospital patiently explained all bedsheets in the maternity ward are routinely incinerated.

At 10 Downing Street, Prime Minister Margaret Thatcher took time off from her bitter battle with the striking miners to remember there was still, symbolically, a greater office than hers, and sent a congratulatory telegram to both Charles and the Queen. As Harry settled down to his first night at Kensington Palace, the royal family seemed as safe as the bed in which he slept. The Queen, at the peak of her reign and enjoying massive public support, now knew the bloodline was protected. In Harry, Charles and Diana had the spare, a second son whose unique position, at least as far as being one of the Windsor family was concerned, was to be there for a day that everybody, including he, hoped would never come.

Meanwhile in a leafy country lane in Wiltshire a young press photographer watched as two cars drove into the home of Camilla Parker Bowles. While his wife slept with their newborn child, Charles was back with his mistress.

CHAPTER TWO

Prince Charles's desire to play polo that weekend had more to do with seeing Camilla Parker Bowles than any sporting inclinations. Ever since he had gone back to his mistress, the prince conducted the affair among the super-rich polo set. Hidden among the wealth and machismo of his fellow players Charles found an understanding oligarchy that would never risk compromising their position and status by telling tales out of school. Indeed among the titled gentry and foreign aristocracy that were Charles's polo-playing friends he found willing conspirators who kept mistresses in the same way they kept polo ponies. In most cases they found the women cost marginally less than the horses.

Thus, private houses, wealthy estates, even holiday homes were made available to the prince and his mistress to indulge their affair without the slightest chance of Diana, or more importantly the press, finding out. So things go in the polo world, where a daughter's hand in marriage can still be exchanged for titles and land, and deliberate losses on the field can be compensated with huge financial deals off it.

Alone at Kensington Palace with her newborn baby, Diana heard on the radio how her husband had scored a hat-trick in his team's victory over Laurent Perrier. After the match, the report said, John Kidd, the captain of the opposition, presented Charles with a magnum of champagne and a large Havana cigar. Despite the wealth and privilege of being a member of the world's most famous monarchy, and despite the joy of her second child's birth, Diana felt like the loneliest person in the world. But she knew that, like his brother, Harry would always be there for her.

Though Harry was third in line to the throne after he was born, it is unlikely he will maintain that position throughout his life. There are two main hereditary positions behind the Queen in the monarchy, the heir apparent and the heir presumptive. The heir apparent is the next in line to the throne, whose right to succeed cannot be defeated by the birth of someone with a superior right to succeed. The eldest son of the reigning sovereign is always the heir apparent, and were he to die, his eldest son would become heir apparent. Thus, Prince Charles is heir apparent to the Queen. If, as is highly possible, he were to predecease her, his eldest son, Prince William would become heir apparent.

The heir presumptive (currently Prince William, but a title

that would come Harry's way if the Queen were to die before William has any children of his own), by contrast, is the next in line to the throne whose right to succeed could be defeated by the birth of someone with a superior right. Thus the Queen, when she was Princess Elizabeth, was heir presumptive from 1936 to 1952, since King George VI might at any time have produced a son who would automatically have become heir apparent.

The news of Harry's birth was treated with tremendous joy at Althorp, the home of his other grandfather, Earl Spencer. Indeed the Earl was so excited he launched a week of celebrations with the enthusiasm of a Roman emperor proclaiming the games open. In a spontaneous burst of joy on first hearing the news, the Earl shouted excitedly from the balcony at Althorp just as the last of the day's visitors were finishing their tour of the historic house. He then ordered the family flag be raised. After retiring to his office the Earl phoned virtually everyone he knew, including a somewhat bemused landlord at The Duke Of York pub in Windsor, who to this day doesn't know why. He also rang several journalists with such wonderful and genuine copy as 'I'm sure Harry will be a very good chap.' Eventually the Earl ran out of people to ring so went down to the staff kitchen in search of a new face to gush the wonderful news too. On a more practical note the Earl invested half a million pounds for Harry. The money, which is worth something like £3 million today, goes to Harry in three stages: at 18, 25 and 40 years of age.

Not so excited about the birth of Harry was Britain's only

communist paper, *The Morning Star*. They recorded the birth and the full name of the prince in seven lines at the bottom of page 5, proving even the comrades liked to keep abreast of what the enemy was up to, though felt no need to celebrate the event.

By the time Harry was five weeks old, he weighed 8 pounds and 10 ounces. 'Everything is absolutely fine,' said Diana, who had decided Harry was now old enough to sit for his first official family portrait. He wore a white cotton gown with lace edging at the sleeves. The picture was taken by that old royal favourite, Harry's great-uncle Lord Snowdon, at Kensington Palace.

The photographs were among the best Snowdon had ever taken. One picture perfectly captured how relaxed William and Harry were together. Both of the boys are barefoot as Harry lies in William's arms. So secure and content was Harry he nearly fell asleep during the shoot, announcing his intentions with a huge yawn that had his parents in fits of laughter as Lord Snowdon worried his subject may not stay awake long enough to be photographed.

Harry was christened Henry Charles Albert David on 21 December in St George's Chapel, Windsor Castle. The ceremony was conducted by the Archbishop of Canterbury, Dr Robert Runcie. For most families, a christening is a uniquely happy occasion; a celebration that brings together relatives and friends without the undue pressure of a wedding or the misery of a funeral. Christenings are embarrassed shuffling in ill-fitting suits in church, cheese and ham rolls in the grandparents' parlour with tinned beer, piano playing and children running underfoot putting sugar in the lager. But the royal family is anything but normal and Harry's christening was marred by a run-in between Princess Diana and her erstwhile sister-in-law, Princess Anne.

It went something like this: Prince Charles was godfather to Anne's son Peter and was keen to repay the honour. His suggestion that Anne be godmother to Prince William had been flatly rejected by Diana, so he, somewhat optimistically, suggested she be godmother to Harry instead. Princess Diana would not entertain the idea. Apart from anything else, Andrew Parker Bowles, the husband of Camilla, was godfather to Anne's daughter, Zara. Despite Charles's pleading, she refused outright and instead snubbed Anne by choosing Lady Celia Vestey, Lady Sarah Armstrong Jones, daughter of Princess Margaret, and Carolyn Bartholomew, her former flatmate.

Prince Charles was allowed to nominate his brother Andrew as godfather, bringing some tongue-in-cheek references to the *Godfather* movies from the Duke of York, along with royal artist Bryan Organ and Gerald Ward, a rich polo player whose mother, the society beauty Susan Corbet, created a scandal in the sixties by having an affair with a Spanish Ambassador who had the rather splendid name of the Marquis Miguel Primo.

The announcement of Harry's godparents sparked an enormous and furious row within the royal family who were not used to being insulted in this way. Prince Philip was so angry that his only daughter had been passed over again as a godparent he refused to speak to Charles or visit Harry for six weeks. Andrew, by now looked upon as a fellow conspirator by the Duke, escaped his father's wrath on the golf course and in the arms of his one true love Koo Stark.

The Queen, possibly looking into the abyss already, tried to compensate Anne by promising her a new royal title (she eventually made her Princess Royal, the highest honour a sovereign can bestow on a female member of the royal family), but the final act in this particularly distasteful family drama was delivered by Anne herself. She was so humiliated by the snub that she declined to even attend the christening, choosing instead to organise a shooting party. In vain the Queen begged Anne to attend, even moving the christening from Buckingham Palace to Windsor in an attempt to be nearer Anne's home, but to no avail. The Princess Royal is not a woman to change her mind once it is made up. When Her Majesty pointed out Anne's absence at the event would be seen as a show of petulance by the press, she merely retorted, 'So what?' and sent her two children, Peter and Zara, instead.

Anne's petulance backfired badly, however. Despite being virtually begged to attend the event by the Queen's private secretary, Michael Shea, she would not change her mind. It was again pointed out to Anne that the world's press would see it as a snub to Diana who was, at the time, far more popular than even the Queen. Anne refused to see sense and consequently was buried by the tabloids. The Murdoch press in particular openly began asking for the first time what exactly it was Princess Anne did to warrant her royal status. It was a beating from which the errant princess never fully recovered. To this day she is still ridiculed in the press for the slightest misdemeanour.

CHAPTER THREE

The first home Harry knew was Highgrove, the beautiful country house his parents had lived in since their marriage. The house was purchased by the Duchy of Cornwall in 1980, specifically for the Prince and Princess of Wales to use as their private country house. Built in 1796 by noted architect John Paul Paul, the house has four reception rooms, nine main bedrooms, a nursery wing and staff quarters. It was owned at the time of purchase by Maurice Macmillan, son of the former Prime Minister Harold Macmillan.

Highgrove is situated near the market town of Tetbury, Gloucestershire. Despite top security, Highgrove is unusually accessible for a royal home. The front entrance sits on the curve of a main road and there is no discernible police presence. The main doorway can also be seen from an adjacent field that, despite being on private property, is frequently invaded by tourists hoping for a quick royal glimpse. The pathway of the field is also well used by the paparazzi. Originally, when Prince Charles brought the house, the front could be seen from the road, but in 1982 two enormous ornamental gates were presented to Charles and Diana as a wedding present from the people of Tetbury, and these, along with some strategically placed trees and bushes, gave the family some privacy from passing motorists and groups of tourists from America and Japan, who would break away from their European tour schedules to make the trip down from London.

Unfortunately for the tourists, they were discouraged straight away from hanging around the main gates. Apart from the security implications, they would have been in serious danger of being run down. Ironically, those that did manage to hang around would wave at the car carrying Diana and the boys through the gates without realising they were only popping into the nearby town to buy sweets where they would be on view to everyone.

The Duchy of Cornwall also owns the surrounding estate, which includes Highgrove Farm. The farm, fringed by woods, surrounds the main house and stands in around 900 acres of land. The actual farming is carried out by the Duchy of Cornwall, under instruction from Prince Charles who, as Chair of its Steering Committee, prepares and sets all farming policy on the Home Farm. Highgrove is run as a commercial enterprise whenever possible, and has been singled out for praise by green groups for its environmentally friendly approach to farming. Straw is never burned, chemical fertilisers are reduced as much as possible and, in keeping with the Cotswold landscape, over 500 metres of dry-stone walls have been rebuilt around the ground. In the early eighties, encouraged by Charles, a decision was made to go organic on three blocks of land. The move was part of a general inclination towards what has since been described as biologically sustainable farming linked directly to conservation, and it was an issue that won Prince Charles a great deal of support from the general public.

When Harry and William were allowed into the farm fields they would often play a daring game that involved racing into the cows' field and shouting at the tops of their voices to make the animals run away. It was not a game the farm hands found very amusing, aware as they were that the beef herd based at Highgrove includes precious pedigree stock, including Aberdeen-Angus females and yearlings, Angus bulls and Angus Friesian cows. Also sharing the permanent green pasture with the beef herd is a flock of Masham and Mule sheep. Among the assorted other livestock are Prince Charles's polo ponies, which spent the winter at Highgrove before returning to Windsor for the polo season. All of the land on Highgrove Farm is kept under constant surveillance from a police observation post adjoined to a farm building. Beneath the main house a cellar has been converted into an elaborate bombproof shelter that is out of bounds to anyone unless an emergency situation arises.

Following Harry's birth both Prince Charles and Diana cut back considerably on their official obligations and duties.

They were determined the children would spend their early years with both parents present. Charles, who is said to have had something of a difficult childhood, and Diana, who knew the pains of divorce and separation, were both united on this.

The family's London home was Kensington Palace. Of all the royal residences this is the most interesting in terms of its history. In 1689, it was bought by William III from the then Secretary of State, the Earl of Nottingham, because the king – who suffered from chronic asthma – was desperate to move from the rambling Palace of Whitehall, situated on the River Thames. He was initially attracted to KP, then known as Nottingham House, by its location, buried as it was in the rural retreat of Kensington, where the air was purer, and yet Parliament and the Palace of Westminster were still accessible.

The palace may well have still been called Nottingham House today had it not been for an unfortunate incident in 1760, when King George II died there in the toilet. A name change was felt necessary in order to free the palace of its associations with this less-than-dignified incident. In the public consciousness, the name Nottingham House would be forever linked to the image of a monarch lying dead in a toilet. Clearly this was not a desirable state of affairs.

KP, as it is now known among members of the royal family, became the much-favoured residence of successive sovereigns. Queen Victoria, in particular, loved the place. She was born and bought up there and her deep affection for her first home saved it from demolition when it began to fall apart during the second half of the nineteenth century. Even more beloved of KP was King George V who once threatened to demolish Buckingham Palace (which he hated) and with the money rebuild Kensington Palace as the main royal residence in London.

Soon after their marriage, Charles and Diana moved into the newly refurbished apartments 8 and 9, which, at the time, had not been inhabited for 40 years. On their first night together at KP, Charles told Diana the legendary story of the ghost of the Countess of Granville – the Countess had occupied the apartments until her death in 1938 – which, he said, could sometimes be seen in her rocking chair in one of the bedrooms. It was a story Diana did not pass on to William and Harry. She had been genuinely scared by the tale and some nights covered her ears beneath the covers for fear of hearing the creaking rocking chair.

At KP the two boys, William and Harry, shared a cosy attic room that had been converted into a luxury nursery. The large, comfortable room was painted a soft yellow. All of the furniture was hand-painted with colourful animals and cartoon characters. The children's meals were served in the nursery and Diana would often join them, especially for afternoon tea. When the family spent the weekend at Kensington Palace, both Charles and Diana would attend a special 'tea' that William would put on, stoically ignoring the year-old Harry's constant screaming and refusal to stop chucking jelly and trifle. Despite their marriage difficulties, both Charles and Diana would look back on these days as among the happiest of their lives.

The walls of the nursery were filled with bookcases and

cabinets for the children's toys. In the early years these were bursting with cuddly toys and stuffed animals, but by the time Harry had reached the age of five he had a complete set of lead toy soldiers and a panzer tank. William, showing none of Harry's aggression in his playthings, preferred dinky cars and puzzles, and in later years Monopoly, a game he would play for hours with his mother. On one occasion William complained she only ever seemed to show an interest in the final quarter of the board that included Bond Street, Oxford Street and Park Lane. At the foot of each bed was a wooden chest filled with more cuddly toys. One of them was a stuffed snoopy that Harry had purloined from his mother's bedroom and refused to give back. The nursery also boasted a wooden rocking horse, a special present from America's then first lady, Nancy Reagan.

Although it is located in the centre of London, Kensington Palace is unusually private for a royal residence. The entrance is a small passageway alongside the opulent Kensington Garden Hotel and is often missed by the innocent tourist. Charles and Diana's apartment boasted a rooftop garden that was often used for family barbecues. Princess Diana would also discreetly take off her clothes for some nude sunbathing throughout the exhaustively hot summers of 1989 and 1990. She stopped this after it was pointed out that her naked body was on show to the residents of the top floors of the Kensington Garden Hotel next door.

Diana loved Kensington Palace and it came as no surprise when, during divorce negotiations in later years, she refused to even consider moving out, despite being offered a number of royal houses in the Belgravia area. At one point Prince Charles offered her £5 million to go house hunting with, but it was pointed out that £5 million might just about cover the costs of making any new house secure for royal inhabitants.

Despite their royal status Princess Diana was determined her children would be brought up 'in the real world' as she called it. She wanted them to interact with other children in a normal social environment; she wanted them to enjoy burgers from fast food joints and not just specially prepared gourmet meals from the palace kitchens. But most of all she wanted them to have fun before they were old enough to understand that there was a harsh, brutal world outside the palace walls that one day William, with his brother's support, would have to rule.

The only real area of dispute Charles and Diana had over the raising of the children was about when they should be told of their royal status. Perhaps surprisingly, it was Diana who wanted the boys to learn as early as possible what destiny had already decided for them, especially William. Charles was against the idea, reminding Diana of how he himself had felt such enormous pressure as a very young child when he realised he would one day be king. Diana eventually agreed with Charles, but asked him to stop calling William 'Wee Willy Wompkins', as she felt he was getting a little old for that now.

At this time, by the mid-eighties, Princess Diana's popularity was at its peak and she was beginning to assert herself within the royal family. Her natural charm and warmth when meeting thousands of members of the public had taught her there was more to being a royal than merely opening hospitals and attending garden parties. Suffering from the collapse of her marriage and gnawed at by the fact her husband was back with his mistress, Diana discovered a natural empathy with the underprivileged, and began to take on more jobs involving the poor and the sick. By searching for kinship with disadvantaged people, Diana was to change the face of the British monarchy forever. While enjoying and admiring Diana's work, the public became aware of other royals, who seemed to be paid enormous amounts of money simply because they were related to the Queen.

As much as she could, Diana would involve both her children in this work. Though she knew it was difficult for them to actually attend official functions, she would discuss the plight of the needy and the sick with them in long family talks after supper. Often Prince Charles would join the family during these talks, noting with pride and satisfaction how successful Diana's methods were. Both boys loved to talk, but it was Harry who, aged four, saw his first condom in an AIDS advert and declared, 'It looks like a maggot skin,' forcing both parents to suppress immediate giggles.

It is not surprising that, during a conversation with an estate worker at Sandringham after her separation from Prince Charles, Diana looked back on these days as among the happiest of her life. 'When the boys were very young,' she said, 'I just remember life being one long laugh whenever they were there.'

Of all the dreams she had for her children, most of all Diana wanted her boys to grow up with an awareness that not everyone was born into a world of wealth and privilege like members of the royal family, another revolutionary move that both angered and frightened any number of royal hangers-on. Even cynical members of the royal court acknowledge that Diana's approach was a staggering success. Both William and Harry grew up with a firm grasp of the social problems of Great Britain and their report cards at successive schools consistently referred to their caring manners and consideration for others. Such comments were the joy of Diana's life. She kept all her sons' report cards in a private box at Kensington Palace and would often take them out to show friends and visitors.

When he was aged eight, Harry overheard his mother discussing the plight of the besieged citizens of Sarejevo with members of the British Red Cross at KP. He immediately volunteered to accompany an aid convoy to the former Yugoslavia, which had been ripped apart by war. Both his parents tactfully pointed out eight years of age was a little young for members of the royal family to be heading off for the carnage of the Balkans.

Diana was aware her children were growing up fast but remained determined their childhoods would know only laughter. Whatever the problems with their marriage, both Charles and Diana went out of their way to avoid any scenes in front of the children, calling an ersatz truce whenever the children were home. But this was one of the few areas of bringing up the boys in which they were not entirely successful. Both Harry and William, with the natural instincts of children, were aware that Mummy and Daddy did not always get along.

It will probably never been known what effect the disintegration of their parents' marriage had on William and Harry, but staff at Highgrove remember watching the boys huddle together on the stairs covering their ears with their hands as Charles and Diana had a raging row in their bedroom. The situation was worse for William, who had seen the disintegration of his parents' marriage from the very start. Prince Charles was reduced to tears one night when he overheard Harry ask his brother how 'bad' it was (the arguments between his parents). William had simply replied, 'Bad!' That incident contributed to the reconciliation Charles and Diana effected before her death.

Both William and Harry enjoyed hundreds of fun-packed trips with their mother throughout the time they spent at KP. One day they would be spotted munching burgers at McDonalds, the next visiting Santa at London's Selfridges or Harrods. And Diana never asked for any privileges when she took the boys to these establishments, despite the management wanting her to. At one Burger King restaurant, Diana ticked off a manager who offered to open a till that wasn't being used, just for her. 'No, thank you, we'll queue like everybody else,' Diana said frostily, before adding, 'Why don't you open it for the other people who are waiting?'

Being offered the chance to jump a queue was something of a peeve to Diana, who knew the quickest way to be branded a phoney by the public was to exploit her royal status and jump to the head of any line. On every public occasion, Diana would insist her children queue with everyone else. She would also dress them in a way unlike any royal child who had been seen in public before. Gone were the traditional, cute, sailors' outfits or matching suits that were usually associated with royal children. Both William and Harry would be dressed casually in jeans and sweatshirts with American-style baseball caps perched precariously on their young heads, with the peaks facing backwards in one of the more ludicrous fashion quirks that so dominated the late eighties. Diana herself would often be seen out in the same clothing, right down to the cap, unfortunately opening herself up to ridicule by a large number of Fleet Street columnists who seemed to forget their vindictive and hurtful remarks after she died.

Still only in her twenties, and remarkably fit, Diana also proved a wonderful goalkeeper for the football matches the boys enjoyed on the lawn at Kensington Palace. Jumping for balls with all the agility of a professional she would constantly thwart William and Harry's attempts to score, often ending up tangled in the net after a particularly spectacular dive. And it wasn't just football that allowed Diana to show off her athleticism. On one occasion Prince William wanted to know if there were any conkers in the trees around KP which he could take to school. Diana knew just the place, so, she led her two children out to the rear garden. Bare-legged, in a blue denim mini-skirt and white tee shirt, she found a ladder in the garage and propped it up against a huge chestnut tree. Hitching up her skirt and revealing a glimpse of thigh, she began to climb up into the branches. Unfortunately, the ladder was not high enough to reach the larger conkers, so Diana ordered a police Range Rover be parked under the tree and the ladder placed on top. She then went back up the

ladder and, to William's great delight, began to throw down
the largest conkers, some of them aimed suspiciously close to
the heads of the large group of police officers who had been
helpful with instructions while looking up her skirt.

But for all the trips to theme parks and Burger King, and all
the attempts by Diana to show her sons how normal people
live, nothing could escape the fact they were still fantastically
rich. Diana, as a mother, did not mean to spoil her children,
she was simply in a situation where they could have anything
they wanted. What mother wouldn't treat her children to a
fantastic multi-purpose TV screen, or the latest computer, if
money were no object? Thus, William and Harry continued to
enjoy the prosperity of the eighties, as endless technological
breakthroughs flooded the market with hi-tech computer
games that quickly found their way to Kensington Palace,
usually delivered in a Harrods van. Diana and her children
also gained entry to a number of major events due to the
privilege of their royal status. Wimbledon and the FA Cup
final were all enjoyed by William and Harry without the
required, and much sought after, tickets.

Family holidays were spent abroad luxury yachts floating
past the most beautiful beaches and lagoons on the
Mediterranean and Caribbean coasts, their hosts usually
members of Europe's ever-dwindling royalty or multi-
millionaire business friends of their father. King Juan Carlos
of Spain and his beautiful wife Sophie were regular hosts on
the Spanish Island of Majorca. William, in particular, found
Juan Carlos fascinating. As the elder son he was allowed to sit
with the men at the end of the long evening meals and listen

to the complex political discussions Charles and Juan Carlos enjoyed over brandy and cigars.

Other holidays, spent on the royal estates such as Sandringham and Balmoral, would be spent indulging in the upper class's favourite pastime of killing animals. Harry in particular was a natural at shooting and was allowed to accompany his father grouse shooting at the relatively young age of nine. Once, William teased his younger brother after Harry had missed a grouse at point-blank range, and badly bruised his shoulder in the process. Rubbing his bruised shoulder, 12-year-old Harry sniffed he would have had the bird if the damn thing hadn't flown off. 'Maybe it's your vision,' William chided, 'have you thought of having your eyes examined?' William continued ragging Harry by telling him that at his age he had already bagged fifteen pheasants in one morning.

Another cause for constant teasing by William concerned the ancient, and somewhat ludicrous, tradition of 'blooding', whereby a youngster killing his or her first animal is smeared in the face with the blood of the victim. William had been 'blooded' in October 1996 when he was 14. After killing his first stag, a magnificent creature that was actually twice the size of the young prince, hunting guides daubed his face in the animal's blood. Prince Charles looked on in pride and was glad his son did not react to the ritual in the same way as his mother had. When Diana was 'blooded', aged 13, also after killing a stag, she fled the field in tears and vowed never to hunt again.

When Harry was 11, a disaster nearly occurred when,

during a shoot on the Queen's estate at Sandringham, he rashly fired at a low-flying bird and missed a helper's head by inches. The moment was captured on film by the ever-present paparazzi, and, for some time after, Harry was reduced to being a 'beater' on hunts until his grandfather, the Duke of Edinburgh, took matters into his own hands and bought Harry a shotgun for Christmas. Princess Diana, who hated guns, was heard to wonder aloud, 'What next ... a tank?'

Balmoral Castle was becoming more and more of an educational experience for both William and Harry. Each time they visited the huge estate, they had a feeling of going back in time to a world most people only read about in biographies of Queen Victoria and her soulmate, Albert. Tea would be poured from the same pot Victoria herself had used. Dinner, always precisely at 8.30pm, was served from silver salvers by liveried footmen who wore red waistcoats decorated with shiny brass buttons.

The social highlights of the Balmoral season included the two Ghillies Balls, given by the Queen for the benefit of her estate workers and some handpicked, favoured locals. In the nearby town of Balatar, those not invited to the Queen's ball have their own celebration at the local church hall. On one occasion it was infiltrated by members of the paparazzi who managed to pass themselves off as members of the Royal Protection Squad and then spent the entire evening hearing locals explain the many obstacles they had arranged to thwart the press on tomorrow's hunt. The paps smiled at this; they hadn't even known there was to be a hunt the following day.

William and Harry, like their father and grandfather, wore

their tartans and kilts to these affairs, their dress perfectly complementing the stunning dresses with Stuart sashes and tiaras that the ladies, including the Queen, would wear as they flounced around the room trying to remember the correct, and complicated, steps to the Highland Fling.

But Balmoral is not easy to an outsider, and William and Harry remained on their best behaviour, aware, like so many before them, that though Balmoral is the one castle where the Queen can let her hair down, there are a rigid set of rules and ancient traditions to be adhered to. Many of these can be confusing to the first-time visitor. Diana herself admitted to being terrified the first time she went there. If a young lady born on the Queen's estate at Sandringham can be daunted by the prospect of a visit to Balmoral, Lord knows how hard it would be for an outsider.

Balmoral is the personal and private property of the Queen, unlike the other royal palaces, which belong to the state. Each year the castle is the venue for the Queen's summer holiday. Arriving in August and staying through to September, Her Majesty is frequently joined by other members of the royal family, who enjoy the total seclusion and the fact that, buried within the thousands of acres of prime Scottish highland, they are far out of sight of the prying lenses of the press. Thus, Balmoral is one of the few places the Queen and her family can be totally relaxed.

From his earliest visits, Harry has long been in love with Balmoral, despite the fact his mother hated the place and would often leave her sons with Charles and head south for some therapeutic shopping. In the early morning mist Harry would walk with his father across miles of fields talking endlessly and excitedly about the shooting and hunting to come. Charles would put his arm around Harry and smile when his son asked him innocent, childish questions he knew that being a father was all about such precious moments.

But it was at Highgrove that Harry really began his childhood. His earliest memories are of playing in the walled garden his father had created within the grounds. While Prince Charles pottered around the garden, Harry would sit for hours on the ground with a miniature set of garden tools and emulate his father by digging small holes in the dirt and talking to the plants. He would also talk to himself, never realising Prince Charles had stopped what he was doing to listen to the one-sided conversations, sometimes clamping his hand across his mouth to prevent laughter. Harry's tool kit, comprising a fork, trowel and rake, was a hand-me-down from his elder brother, who, despite his father's encouragement, had not taken a shine to gardening, preferring instead to stay indoors with his mother. It had not gone unnoticed among royal staff that already Harry and William, though aged just three and five, were each spending more time with a different parent.

For Harry those gardening days were happy ones. He especially loved the summer evenings when, after a frantic bout of soiling and digging, Charles and Harry would retire to a garden bench with a bottle of orange squash. Then, as the dusk settled and the creeping darkness came across the fields, they would talk, Harry willing the light to stay, which meant he could spend more time with his father.

Then, when he was five years old, Harry first saw the movie *Zulu*. In Great Britain, this particular movie is considered a masterpiece. The story, of a small band of British soldiers who managed to defeat thousands of Zulu warriors at Rorke's Drift in South Africa in 1879, is shown every year and, like British tennis players at Wimbledon, never fails to raise an audience, despite the fact everyone knows what's going to happen.

Harry loved the film and questioned his father extensively about Rorke's Drift. In particular he was fascinated to learn of the regiments who took part in the siege. As Prince of Wales, Charles was aware of the South Wales Borderers, and promised Harry he would one day take him to the regiment's home base. In fact Charles was only half able to deliver his promise. When Harry was ten he visited the Royal Engineers, the second regiment involved at Rorke's Drift, as the South Wales Borderers had long since been disbanded.

Harry's thirst for knowledge about the whole *Zulu* campaign eventually led to an interest in all matters military. He was fortunate in that his family had more than their fair share of military connections: his father is Colonel-in-Chief of 12 regiments, possibly giving him more uniforms than action man; his grandfather was a war hero and remains a Field Marshall in the British, Australian and New Zealand armies; and his grandmother is head of all Britain's armed forces and the only person in the country who can officially declare war and peace.

As a small child Harry would interrogate the various members of the royal family who had military careers. In particular he loved talking to Prince Andrew, who served as a helicopter pilot during the Falklands war. He would also talk to his grandfather of the Duke's adventures during the war and his exploits with the legendary Lord Mountbatten. He did not talk much to his other uncle, Edward. It is considered not very tactful in the royal family to mention Prince Edward's stint in the Marines, which was about as successful as the *Titanic*'s maiden voyage.

But Harry's great love was the Parachute Regiment and, after being given a replica uniform in 1986, he informed his mother and father he intended to make this his career when he left school. The news was welcomed by Prince Charles, who had earned his wings with a number of parachute jumps, but Princess Diana wasn't so enthusiastic, especially when, some years later, her lover James Hewitt let slip that the life expectancy of a Para in battle is about four minutes.

Harry's interest in the military combined with his fascination with history that began at a very early age. Again he was lucky to be surrounded by history, living history in the Queen Mother's case. He became obsessed with his own name and devoured books on the Henrys of the royal family. There were many, as Henry has always been a popular name with the royal family, and with Shakespeare. The name dates back to the twelfth century and King Henry I, the son of William the Conqueror. For some reason, young Harry, reading long into the hot summer nights at Highgrove, relished the story of King Henry II, who ordered the murder of Thomas a Becket in Canterbury Cathedral. He also discovered Shakespeare through his father reading selected passages from *Henry V*, and *Henry IV Parts One and Two*. And he loved the rousing battleground speech in *Henry V* that ends, 'Cry, "God for Harry! England and St George!"' a quote he was to use with much mirth some years later when he was entertaining the Spice Girls. King Henry VII was the only English king actually crowned on the battlefield, and a character much admired by the younger prince. Yet Harry was, and remains, indifferent to history's most famous Henry, Henry VIII, despite being amused by the fact that Henry VIII had the largest codpiece in the Tower of London. However, the idea that a reigning monarch should have his wives' heads chopped off simply because he wanted to marry another woman filled the young Harry with horror.

Life at Highgrove was idyllic for Harry in his early years. He worshipped his elder brother William and would emulate his every movement to the great amusement of his parents. If William lay on the floor and put one foot in the air, so would Harry. When William ran around the kitchen table shouting at the top of his voice, unfortunately for everyone within earshot, so did Harry.

Both boys loved the outdoor life that the enormous amount of land at Highgrove gave them. They learned about life on the farm by watching the lambs being sheared and taken off to auction. Neither boy was squeamish when it came to nature's more ruthless side. William, in particular, had a child's morbid fascination with dead animals and, like their mother before them, the boys would carry out elaborate funerals when they discovered a dead rodent.

William would never forget where a grave was. Once, when

he was five and out walking with Diana and Harry, he dug up a rabbit's grave and pulled the badly decomposed carcass out. To Diana's horror, and Harry's squeals, he then raised the dead rabbit above his head and began to swing it round. His mother ordered him to 'put that bloody thing down NOW', but William only swung it harder, threatening to launch it at Diana if she came any closer. The rabbit was eventually thrown on to a compost heap but re-buried a few days later, again by William and Harry. They also showed a strange interest in the magpie trap, a contraption designed to lure the birds and catch them so they could be destroyed en masse. William and Harry both took great delight at peering in on the condemned birds as they awaited execution.

Both Charles and Diana were determined their children would enjoy a normal family life, so weekends were always spent at Highgrove unless royal duties prevented the arrangement. On Saturday mornings, William would rise early and toddle down the hall to Diana's room. Usually he was accompanied by a very sleepy Harry and the pair of them would jump into Diana's bed. On one occasion Harry bounced off the bed and landed with a crash on the bedside table, scattering the large collection of photographs Diana always kept there and breaking two of the glass frames. As the two princes were so young it had not occurred to either of them that it was unusual for their parents not to sleep together. On the one time they did question the sleeping arrangements at Highgrove, Charles told them Mummy could not stand the sound of his snoring. This was readily accepted by the boys, and there was some truth in it: when their parents had slept together, he would often find Diana's earplugs in the bed.

But behind the scenes all was not well. By the time of Harry's first birthday, in September of 1985, Charles and Diana's marriage was over in all but name and yet, to their credit, they managed to keep up a united front for the children's sake. When they were at Highgrove the weekends were devoted to the boys. Prince Charles was desperate for his young sons to enjoy the countryside as much as he did. He knew they would be expected to hunt and shoot with the rest of the royal family and introduced them to as many rural activities as their young ages would allow.

At a very early age Prince William had shown a natural ability at riding horses, a skill heartily encouraged by his father. With Harry watching, Prince William would be led around the Highgrove grounds on either Smokey or Trigger, his two ponies. Sometimes Harry, aged just 14 months, would be allowed to sit in the saddle alongside his brother, but the tears would flow when he was told he could not actually ride the horse himself. To make matters worse, William had begun to show off on his ponies whenever Harry was watching. William had first been introduced to horse riding at the age of three when he would be led around the paddock on a leading rein. However, he soon became tired of riding around at a snail's pace and was trying to trot and canter before he had learned the basic art of controlling a pony. By the age of seven, William had become a competent horseman, vaulting on and off his bareback pony with ease and even riding his sturdy

Shetland pony standing on the saddle, much to Harry's amusement and the concern of his minder.

Unlike William, Harry had begun to show a boisterous curiosity that at times bordered on the dangerous. Whether it was digging up ants' nests in the Highgrove garden or taunting a billy goat on the farm, he was forever causing concern for his minder who would invariably try to stay in front of him and anticipate the mayhem to come rather than follow behind at a safe distance. As one police minder once remarked, 'There was no safe distance with Harry ... The combined armies of NATO don't have the destructive force of Harry on a mission to cause mischief.'

At the time one of Prince William's favourite games was to create a roadblock on the estate and force staff and police to pay a toll to pass. Already showing a protective maturity beyond his five years, William would prevail upon Harry not to start throwing stones at those people who did not have the 50p fee on them. Harry was oblivious to danger and liked nothing better than to run into the field at Highgrove Farm and chase the cows. Once, a cow that was being chased by Harry headed towards a panicking Princess of Wales who, to both her children's amusement, ignobly launched herself over a fence. Through his laughter Harry pointed out that Diana had ripped her green parka.

From a very early age Harry was determined to carry out his first parachute jump. His first experiment in freefalling led to the first of many injuries sustained throughout his childhood. Standing on the table of the Highgrove kitchen, Harry suddenly launched himself off in a highly detailed impersonation of a para about to land. Unfortunately as he hit the floor his momentum carried him forward and he smashed his head against the table. The injury was sufficiently serious to need stitches. In vain did members of the royal family try to hide Harry's injury and newly acquired scar just after the incident at the wedding of Prince Andrew and Fergie. Harry proudly showed the blemish to everyone. His mother referred to it as 'his first war wound'.

CHAPTER FOUR

On a sunny day in September 1985, Prince William began his first day at school. After much discussion his parents had decided on Mrs Mynor's Nursery School in Notting Hill Gate. The venue was chosen for its close proximity to Kensington Palace and the fact it wasn't entirely populated by the wealthy. Diana in particular looked forward to idle gossip with the other mothers and taking part in the 'school run', that great bane of England's commuters where middle-class mothers drive their 2.6 children to school while chatting on their mobile phones, oblivious to other drivers.

Mrs Mynor's Nursery was a friendly, happy school with three classes of 12 pupils. On his first day, William, accompanied by his mother and wearing a bright red pair of shorts and checked shirt, hardly blinked at the waiting photographers, who assumed, incorrectly, he was merely nervous about his first day at school. William's main concern, however, had been an emotional scene at KP earlier that morning when Harry, just days after his first birthday, had let loose a torrent of tears on being told he would be separated from his brother for the whole morning. The scene had upset Princess Diana as well, who had not realised how close Harry had become to his brother, and how he could not bear to be parted from him, to the extent that he would often crawl into bed with William late at night. In fact Harry and William were separated two mornings each week, and each time Harry would be reduced to tears. Eventually his mother allowed Harry on the school run so he could spend precious more moments with his elder brother. On one occasion Harry, accompanied by both his parents, saw William act in the school's nativity play. It was the first time he had been allowed to accompany his parents inside William's school. Later, back at Kensington Palace, Harry insisted the event was immediately replayed with him taking on the role of shepherd and Charles as an unlikely inn-keeper.

The carefree family life at KP and Highgrove that Charles and Diana were so determined their children would continue to enjoy was not all plain sailing. When Harry was two, his nanny, Barbara Barnes, left the royal household after daring to question the discipline of the two children in her charge. The older, more experienced woman, was beginning to notice how William in particular did not know where to draw the line between being funny and cute, and being downright rude and disruptive. Whichever way one looked at it, William's behaviour was becoming more and more wild and was not being looked on by Nanny Barnes as the usual petulance of a young child. She began to look on her charge with increasing worry. In particular an incident at a school birthday party had raised eyebrows among senior members of the royal family and caused concern to the other mothers. One of the children at the kindergarten was having a birthday party. All of the children were tremendously excited and launched into the celebrations with the tireless enthusiasm only children can muster at such events that usually mean endless problems for the adults. But William had decided he didn't want to be there and began playing up badly. He refused to sit with the other children and responded to his teacher's protests by throwing his food on the floor, causing the other children to stop playing as the teachers admonished the errant prince. When he was ordered to pick up the mess he defiantly refused and informed the staff, 'When I'm king I'm going to send all my knights around to kill you ...' The words, though childlike in their delivery, were considered sufficiently serious for the incident to be reported to his parents by both the school and William's personal detective.

When Diana was informed of his behaviour she immediately apologised to the other mothers and their children, but Charles was both angry and worried. At home William had by now become quite a handful and already Harry was showing signs of following in his brother's footsteps. Both children would refuse to go to bed at night, and virtually every evening was disrupted by William's tears before bedtime, when he would be summarily marched to his bed by his nanny despite his wailing. On one occasion Diana slapped William hard on the behind, an incident she regretted but was forced to repeat in public that summer when William virtually assaulted a young girl at Windsor Great Park. The ensuing spanking from his mother was captured on film by the press, and the public humiliation the young prince was forced to undergo went a long way to changing his current attitude. Unfortunately the chastisement hurt Diana a great deal and, after viewing the pictures in the following day's papers, she vowed never to hit her children again.

The main problem in the relationship between Diana and Nanny Barnes was their difference of opinion on how two royal princes should be raised. Barnes was a traditionalist and enjoyed being the formal royal nanny. She could not understand why Diana wanted to take such an active part in her own children's upbringing. Most women, she reasoned, would be only too glad to hand their children over to a nanny. The pair were also at odds over what Diana referred to as 'the normal life' she wanted her children to have. An exasperated Nanny Barnes would tell friends, 'It's no good Diana pretending (the boys) can have a completely normal life, because (they) can't.'

Diana would insist the boys were dressed as she wanted and not kitted out in the traditional, cute yet boring clothes that gave them no individuality. Nanny Barnes, who was called 'Baba' by William and Harry, would look on with concern as the holes in their shoes and trousers grew even larger after each day spent playing with Diana. It was not the way young members of the royal family should be dressed, thought Barnes, and led it to a number of words between her and her employer, Diana. The main bone of contention was William's increasingly naughty behaviour, which even the Queen had commented on during a recent visit to Windsor Castle. William had met Her Majesty's frosty disapproval after he went to an old stable block with Harry, not realising a horse was inside. The boys were forbidden to go anywhere near the horses without an adult. Princess Diana held her peace when the Queen admonished William, but found, like an awful lot of other mums, she did not like her mother-in-law telling off her son.

Harry, on the other hand, began to use his brother's antics as a yardstick for his own mischief, even going so far as to make the Queen blush furiously when, during afternoon tea at Windsor, he complimented her Majesty's fashion sense by saying, 'Oooh ... That's a pretty dress!' But not all his antics were quite so cute. One day, as Prince Charles was heading off on an official trip, he walked across the lawn at Highgrove towards a helicopter of the Queen's flight, parked in an adjacent field. Harry, kitted out in full combats, ambushed his father with a death-defying yell as he jumped on his back. Unfortunately for Charles, his youngest son had been frolicking in the muddy fields all morning and liberally covered his father's formal suit in dirt, forcing the somewhat angered prince back indoors for a quick change of suit. Diana could barely suppress the giggles as Harry looked up and innocently asked, 'What have I done wrong now?'

The only 'punishment' William and Harry ever seemed to endure was a trip to the 'woodshed'. In America the expression 'a trip to the woodshed' is filled with horror for most youngsters, as it is traditionally the place where thrashings are carried out by parents on their children. In William and Harry's case, inside the 'woodshed' was a large net, filled with thousands of multi-coloured small plastic balls into which the naughty royal would be thrown. Often Diana or Charles would drench the boys with water fired from high-powered water pistols before hurling them into the shed and, amidst guffaws of laughter, they would be forced to 'swim' through the thousands of balls.

It was fairly obvious to most members of staff that young Harry had learned very early on how to wrap his mother round his little finger simply by crying rather than demanding. Prince Charles, sufficiently concerned about William to have spoken to the Queen about him, was now concerned Harry was turning out the same. On Her Majesty's advice, Charles tentatively broached the subject of replacing the liberal Nanny Barnes with someone who would take a stronger line with both William and Harry. Not surprisingly, Diana was in total agreement. By this time, January 1987, Prince William was ready to move up to his pre-prep school Wetherby, also in Notting Hill, and it was seen as a perfect opportunity for Nanny Barnes to leave without losing too much face.

Diana's motives for removing Barbara Barnes were not entirely based on William's behaviour. Over the past few months she had watched with growing concern as William began to form a close bond with the motherly Barbara. In particular Diana hated the fact that William responded to Nanny Barnes's chastisements whereas with her he simply sulked for hours, knowing she would come bearing gifts and hugs. Barbara Barnes had also formed a close relationship with Harry, who was not told she was leaving for good when she drove out of Kensington Palace in January 1987.

Her replacement was Ruth Wallace, a brisk and businesslike woman who had a tremendous amount of experience with children. She had worked with sick children before becoming nanny to King Constantine of Greece, a close friend of Prince Charles. Both Charles and Diana were convinced she was going to bring a breath of fresh air to William and Harry's lives. The new nanny began work in March 1987 and immediately endeared herself to staff at both Highgrove and KP. The ever-present police officers, mostly men, found her attractive and easy to get along with. She could also enjoy a drink and spent many an evening at Highgrove telling jokes and stories in the staff kitchen.

Nanny Wallace was awarded one important concession Barnes had never enjoyed. Following much discussion between Diana and Charles it was decided she would be allowed to smack both William and Harry. Diana had only agreed to the arrangement after much soul-searching. She herself resolutely refused to smack her children and yet, paradoxically, she was willing to allow another adult to do it. Diana herself admitted to close friends that this was something she could not quite figure out. The arrangement, however, was not a success. In the event, Diana resented another woman chastising her children, and would often demand to know why either Harry or William had been punished. Stroking their tear-stained faces and comforting them, she was secretly pleased she had not been responsible for their pain and was now being looked on as an ally by both the children.

CHAPTER FIVE

In the late summer of 1986, just before Harry's second birthday, a man with a reputation for being a womaniser eased his way into Princess Diana's life and affections. His name was James Hewitt. Emotionally speaking, Hewitt, a serving army officer, could not have happened at a worse time for Diana. She already knew her marriage was falling apart and felt increasingly isolated within the confines of the royal family. Diana was also beginning to suspect that her husband and his courtiers were plotting against her. In fact she saw plots and conspiracies everywhere, even down to an elaborate, and absurd, plot by MI5 to have her declared insane and take her children from her.

The powers that be, within the royal family were watching Diana with mounting concern, convinced she was in the advanced stages of paranoia and quite capable of doing harm to herself. They were also growing increasingly alarmed by Diana's somewhat ludicrous threats to tell the world her marriage was a sham, usually blurted out to Prince Charles as he sought refuge from yet another row. But they were also aware her anger and frustration were not entirely without foundation. In a secret meeting held at Windsor Castle, Prince Charles had already told the Queen and the Duke of Edinburgh he loved Camilla and had made a terrible mistake marrying Diana. Despite evidence to the contrary, Prince Charles does confide in his father, the Duke of Edinburgh, who always insists on being present when his eldest son requests a private meeting with the Queen.

Though his parents sympathised with Charles, he was told in no uncertain terms that divorce was out of the question. Charles was well-versed enough in upper-class double-talk to know this meant he could continue seeing Camilla, but the public, who had so willingly bought into the fairytale of his marriage, must never know the truth, despite the nonsensical threats Diana continued to shout from the battlements. For Charles this was enough. He could indulge in his first love, Camilla, whilst serving his second, the United Kingdom. All things considered, he reflected, things were looking better already. As Charles was leaving Windsor Castle after the meeting, the Queen nonchalantly enquired, 'Does Diana have any men friends?' Charles did not answer, but a look was exchanged between the monarch and her son which suggested life would be an awful lot easier if she did.

Diana's mounting anger came with the realisation that

Charles no longer loved her. In vain she pleaded with Charles to stop seeing Camilla, a request he had no intention of honouring. What Diana did not realise was how hopelessly in love with Camilla her husband was. And she had also forgotten to take into account how totally irrational people are when it comes to love. For now his parents knew of his affair, Charles was acting as if it was Diana who was in the wrong. He believed she should pull herself together and stop behaving in the way that he had always seen her, as a silly little girl. In vain Diana protested it was his actions that were causing so much grief in her life, that she would pull herself together if only he would come back to her. As extraordinary as it seems, despite the pain, despite the hurt, Princess Diana was still in love with Prince Charles.

It is, therefore, not surprising that the hurt and vulnerable Diana should have so easily fallen for Hewitt's silver charm when she met him at a London party in the late summer of 1986. One of Hewitt's lovers, a girl with strong military links, always referred to him as 'the mounted cavalry' and, after a night of sex, compared his performance to 'having been shagged by the entire 17/21st Lancers'.

Diana and Hewitt then began an affair that was to last nearly five years. It was not a particularly happy or passionate affair. Despite Hewitt's later claims that made it sound like the greatest love story of all time, it was never in any danger of rivalling *Wuthering Heights*.

Harry first set eyes on Hewitt at Kensington Palace. Princess Diana had invited her lover to dine at her London home despite the fact her children were there. It was a risk she was prepared to take to satisfy the sexual desires Hewitt had awakened in her. For the first time in her life Diana felt like a sexually attractive woman with a man who took notice of her and she was determined to make the most of it. Harry and William would be taken into their mother's sitting room after their evening baths and introduced to 'Mummy's friend'. Freshly bathed, and wrapped in warm towelling robes, the boys would listen politely as their mother regaled Hewitt with their latest escapades. Hewitt would laugh and encourage Diana to tell more stories, trying to show her how great he was with her boys.

But Hewitt was distinctly uncomfortable in their presence. To him they were a constant, and instant, reminder that his relationship with Diana was ultimately doomed. An army major, currently struggling to make the captain's exam, with little money and no academic qualifications, was hardly going to ride off into the sunset with the Princess of Wales and her two children.

But in the children Hewitt did see the obvious way to remain in Diana's affections. He knew, like anyone else who had ever got close to Diana, that she lived and breathed William and Harry. There was nothing she wouldn't do for them; it was as if her very existence depended on their happiness. William and Harry supplied Diana with the love her husband had deprived her of, and she was addicted to it.

But to Hewitt, William and Harry were the fundamental reason why their love affair was doomed to failure. Diana would leave Charles, he believed, but she would never leave the children. Hewitt wanted Diana's love exclusively, but she would never be prepared to give that. And the love was reciprocated. William and Harry idolised their mother. Whole evenings were spent in front of the TV at Kensington Palace with Harry sprawled in Diana's arms as William sat at her feet, Diana's hand gently stroking his head. It was the same in her bedroom where Diana would sleep with the boys wrapped around her. As they grew older and slept in their own beds, she would will the weather to rain, knowing the slightest hint of thunder would bring the boys to the safety of their mother's bed.

Hewitt had already learned of young Harry's increasing interest in the military. One of Harry's favourite moments had occured recently, when a Cavalry Colonel had bowed to him and addressed him with a resoundingly military-sounding 'SIR' that was so loud it had almost made the three-year-old Harry fall off his tricycle. In a canny move that earned him a large number of brownie points with Diana, Hewitt arranged for the boys to spend the day with the army at Combermere barracks in Windsor. It was a good move. Diana could not wait to tell the children. Hewitt had discovered that, by making Diana's children happy, he made her happy ... it was a tactic he would try to use again and again with predictable results. William and Harry quickly began to loathe him.

But, for that first special treat, the children turned up with their mother in a haze of excitement. Harry, in particular, was thrilled to see a number of tanks at the barracks, just as Prince Charles had told him there would be, and had to be restrained from clambering straight up on to one as soon as he alighted from the car.

Hewitt had arranged for the boys to wear miniature flak-jackets, army trousers and berets. Unfortunately he had to turn down both Harry's and William's requests for a gun, even after William had innocently responded that his dad had let him fire his gun earlier that year. This fact did not amuse Diana, who considered five years old ridiculously young for a child to hold a gun.

The boys were then taken on a guided tour of the barracks that, to Diana's dismay, took in the gun display cabinets. On seeing the vast array of weapons, Harry and William began pleading with their mother to be allowed to play with one of them, William once again reiterating that he knew how to handle a rifle. On seeing her sons' enthusiasm for the weapons she herself hated, Diana made a mental note to have a word with her husband. Hastily, Hewitt arranged for the boys to get a ride in a tank as an alternative, something that made Harry in particular squeal in delight when he realised he was finally going to get into his beloved tank. As Harry was driven back to Highgrove that night he fell fast asleep in the back of the car, the excitement of the day having exhausted him completely.

After this, Hewitt became a regular guest at Highgrove, driving down on those Friday nights when Prince Charles was conveniently away on business, and spending the weekend with Diana. On a number of occasions Harry and William were staying with their mother when Hewitt arrived. They had already begun to resent him. Hewitt was a man who did not take lightly to playing second fiddle to children when competing for a woman's affections, and William, in particular, sensed this. Hewitt's attempts to ingratiate himself with the children were irritating rather than endearing. Neither William nor Harry could completely relax in his presence.

The affair eventually fizzled out in the early nineties. Diana, finally seeing through the painfully transparent Hewitt, ended the affair after Hewitt returned from serving in the Gulf War. It was a particularly cruel homecoming for Hewitt, who had thought he would return to her arms as the war hero he had always wanted to be. Instead her refusal to take his phone call finally opened the eyes of the silver-tongued charmer who, when Diana had told him how much her husband had made her suffer and how terrible it was to be alone, had replied, 'You are not alone … you have me.'

Diana certainly did have him: he hung around until the day she died.

CHAPTER SIX

In September 1987, Harry also started at Mrs Mynor's Nursery School. Unlike William he had not been keen to start kindergarten and his first day at school was somewhat ruined by his tears that morning at KP. Harry clung to his mother throughout the 10-minute journey to the school from KP during which she assured him she too had been terrified on her first day at school. Diana, who well remembered the miserable time she was subjected to at her finishing school in Switzerland, almost gave in at one point and suggested to Harry's personal detective that maybe tomorrow would be a better day to start.

But as soon as Harry saw the waiting throng of press photographers a change seemed to come over him. He leaped from the car and proceeded to make funny faces towards the cameras, much to his mother's obvious joy and amusement. 'Harry, the Clown Prince', as the press immediately dubbed him, loved the audience, and was quite prepared to play up to the cameras, something he does to this day. 'From the moment he got out of the car on that first day we knew he was going to be a star,' says photographer Glenn Harvey, one of Britain's most experienced royal snappers. 'Harry loved the camera. He loved being the centre of attention. In the end they had to drag him into the school. Harry would have stood there having his picture taken all day if his mother hadn't pulled him away.'

On that first day the young prince was referred to simply as 'Harry' by all the staff and pupils. Settling in was not easy. Originally he found himself at something of a loss among the three dozen other pupils. Despite the best attempts of both his parents, Harry did not mix well with the other children. Though he was not old enough to admit it, or even realise it, Harry was desperately missing his elder brother. His reluctance to make friends, however, was put down to his being the new boy, but Diana, with the instincts of a mum, was already voicing concerns that Harry only seemed really happy among others when his brother William was with him.

Eventually, as so often happens, Harry did settle down and even began to show a natural ability as a leader. Many a playtime game found Harry taking charge as his small band of friends was encouraged to play follow the leader – in the most out-of-bounds areas of the school. Diana's concerns had been assuaged by Prince Charles who had told her it was only a matter of time before Harry settled down and made friends.

She hugged herself with delight one morning when she watched Harry lead his friends in some playground games, smiling at how right her husband had been. For two people involved in a bitter marriage it is extraordinary how tuned in Charles and Diana were when it came to their children.

There were three levels of schooling at Mrs Mynor's. The children started as Cygnets, moved up to Little Swans and eventually left the nursery as Big Swans. As well as a basic awareness of numbers and letters of the alphabet, students were encouraged to paint and even make clay sculptures. Harry in particular relished the painting sessions when he could use paints and crayons with wild abandon, never noticing that most of the colour seemed to end up on him and not the white card. He also failed to realise how amusing his antics were to his teachers, who would suppress giggles behind him as he launched another assault on the painting board.

The school also encouraged pupils to take part in the endless plays and concerts they put on for the parents. During the school's nativity play in 1988, Harry stole the limelight when he reprised his role as the shepherd he had played before at KP with his inn-keeper dad and Diana as Joseph. It was his first real taste of stardom and, as he stood on the stage at the end of the play, he relished the audience's applause, noting with pride how enthusiastically his own parents were clapping him.

Of course being a royal schoolboy has special implications, and the time was rapidly approaching when William and Harry would have to learn a little more about the business of being royal. On a bright autumn day in 1988, Prince Harry, by now aged four and about to start at a new school, was driven to Windsor Castle with his brother Prince William. Unusually neither one of their parents was with them. The boys were accompanied by two detectives and their Nanny Wallace for a special treat ... tea with Her Majesty the Queen.

The meeting was not just for fun. Despite the relative young ages of the two princes they were about to begin the most important lessons of their lives in preparation for the day they would actively join the ranks of working members of the royal family. Because of Prince William's unique position (he is one of only two men on earth who will one day sit on the throne of England), he was schooled in royal protocol by the Queen herself. It was decided Harry should accompany his brother not only for company but for practical reasons as well. If anything were to happen to William before he produced a child of his own, Harry would take the crown. Thus the two boys found themselves within the magnificent setting of the Queen's private chambers overlooking the immaculately mown lawns of Windsor Castle, while the monarch discussed what it meant to be royal.

Both William and Harry found these weekly trips enthralling. The Queen was the perfect teacher. The settings were informal, sometimes the Queen would take the boys into her private garden where they would sip lemonade, or they would idly stroll over to the horses' paddock. The princes were intrigued and amazed by the Queen's casual chats with the estate workers, who they would bump into all the time. In particular, they loved the informal relationships Her Majesty maintains with certain, favoured estate workers. Every year the Queen buys her staff a Christmas present. Although the actual gift is bought by a minnow somewhere far down the chain of command, the Queen is kept informed of who got what. On this particular year, one worker, with a reputation for saying what's what, had been given a shirt. When the Queen, fully aware of the gift, had asked how the shirt was, he had told her it was unfortunately the wrong size. 'Oooh dear,' remarked the Queen. 'Well we'd better have it back then and get you a new one.' The shirt was duly handed back and exchanged, a small gesture that created quite an impression on both William and Harry, who realised kindness was not the exclusive domain of their mother.

They also discovered a deep affection for the Duke of Edinburgh who, despite his somewhat aloof public image, enjoys great popularity among his staff. One sunny afternoon, during a particularly gruelling lesson on the English Civil War from his grandmother, Harry was looking out of the window dreaming wistfully of halcyon summer days playing cricket, when the Duke came into view, striding across the castle lawns on his way back from the stables. Looking up, he noticed Harry and, possibly remembering the drudgery of his own school days, immediately embarked on a series of grotesque face-pullings that reduced the young prince to fits of giggles. The Queen, noticing she had lost the attention of one of her pupils, came across to the window to be greeted by the Duke of Edinburgh doing a passable impersonation of Quazimodo. Both boys burst into peals of laughter as the monarch, in no uncertain terms, ordered her husband to clear off.

On 11 September 1989, just four days short of his fifth birthday, Harry joined William at the pre-prep Wetherby School. William had attended Wetherby for two years and was looking forward to being joined by his brother. In many ways William paved the way for a smooth entrance to what was, effectively, Harry's first real school. The school's teachers and pupils were by now quite accustomed to having royalty in their midst and even managed to ignore the ever-present police bodyguards who, no matter how hard they tried, could never quite conceal themselves among a bunch of children.

Harry, at this point in his life, was beginning to lean on William and allow his older brother to take the lead in the voyage of discovery on which the pair had now been launched. It was an intimate friendship they had. Though they were brothers, each was also the other's best mate. It was a bond that was to grow stronger and stronger as they grew until, by their teens, they could literally read each other's minds. If for any reason either of the boys was in trouble and needed a hastily arranged alibi, both knew they could rely on the other without even asking. Memorably, Prince William once went to the stables at Windsor Castle against his mother's wishes. When Diana asked Harry where his brother was, he told her William was playing golf. When a very muddied Prince William got back some time later Diana suggested to Harry that William must have spent a great deal of time in the rough.

Academically Harry was outshining his brother. He was considered highly intelligent by his teachers and was placed in the top group of students at his school. Both Charles and

Diana, though tremendously pleased with Harry's progress, were not entirely surprised that he was overtaking his elder brother. This was no slight on William, who had been in an average group for his first two years at Wetherby, but a reflection of Harry's ever-growing thirst for knowledge. A member of Charles's staff at the time described Harry as 'a walking encyclopaedia – he positively loved learning new things, any scrap of information interested him as long as it was something new'.

The staff member, who is still working for the royal family, said, 'At a very young age William and Harry saw the world differently from each other. To William the world was a complicated place with no room for errors of judgement. He knew he wouldn't be allowed to make mistakes. Therefore William would always look at things from all angles before reaching any decision. Harry was oblivious to this way of thinking. If he wants to do something he just goes straight ahead and does it without giving any consideration to the consequences. That's not to say he is a bad boy, he's not. Harry is one of the nicest people you could ever meet, there is nothing he wouldn't do for anyone. Harry's only problem is that he doesn't always think things out. If Harry wants to make a goal for football he'll knock two bits of wood in the ground as posts ... the fact the wood has just been pilfered from a royal bench doesn't really faze him.' Once, during a visit to Smiths Lawn to watch polo, a detective tried to point out to Harry the dangers of walking in front of on-coming cars. Harry scoffed, 'They're not allowed to knock you down.'

At Highgrove, Prince Charles was forced to ban the boys

go-karting sessions when Harry, aged nine, and William, eleven, would race along the quiet country lanes and across the fields at Highgrove Farm. Their karts could reach speeds of up to 30mph, but Harry was beginning to show worrying signs of a complete disregard for danger. He was also showing an increasing disregard for the basic laws of physics, which suggest go-karts can't go round corners at 30mph. It was the same at Windsor Castle, where the Queen had reluctantly allowed Harry and William permission to bring their go-karts one Easter. Her Majesty was rudely awoken at around 7.30am on Easter Saturday, by the two boys roaring across the pathway that went directly below her bedroom window. Enquiring of her husband, 'What on earth is that noise?' the Duke, still half-asleep, mumbled, 'That's those bloody go-karts you let them bring ...'

After one accident too many, Charles stopped the races and ordered the boys to use the karts only at official public tracks. The news was greeted with enthusiasm by Diana who, also concerned about the obvious dangers of speeding in country lanes, and taking corners at 30mph, was secretly pleased she would now be able to take the boys to London to perform the sport. While they were racing around the countryside Diana could only wait at Highgrove for their return, but by taking them go-karting in London she could have a day out herself.

Quickly she arranged a visit to the professional circuit at Donnington Park. She also called upon motor-racing legend Jackie Stewart to escort Harry around the Silverstone track, something that so thrilled the young prince he excitedly told his mother he now wanted to be a Formula One driver, a statement that sent Diana into fits of worry as racing drivers were being killed at an alarming rate that year. Suddenly a career in the Paras didn't seem so dangerous to Diana.

Harry's growing confidence academically was also helped greatly by the curriculum at Wetherby, which relied heavily on encouraging young minds to express themselves artistically. His favourite lessons were painting and model-making, both of which he had spent long evenings doing with his mother and father and which now gained him high marks. His other love at school was English comprehension. In particular he loved writing stories and was considered by his teachers to be a gifted writer. Prince Charles allowed himself to smile when he read this in a report card and remembered many an evening spent in his personal library at Highgrove with Harry searching for a new book to read. In later years a friend asked Prince Charles why he had several Stephen King novels in his library, as the master of horror stories is hardly Prince Charles's usual reading matter. Charles explained they were Harry's, and that he was forever leaving his books in Charles's library. Prince Charles had also spent many evenings reading to the boys, who would be wrapped in robes after their baths. William would sit obediently on the floor and Harry would sprawl across his father. These were wonderful moments for Charles, who remembered fondly how his own brothers would sit in the same positions as his sons when he had told them the same, familiar stories he now read to his children.

Harry's daily lessons at Wetherby also included basic introductions to foreign languages and computers. He enjoyed the computer, showing a natural aptitude on the keyboard. From an early age both Harry and William had played computer games and had an enormous collection of games and CD-roms such as the *Encyclopaedia Britannica*. But Harry's favourite pastime at school was anything that involved performing, whether this meant singing in the school choir or acting out plays during the drama classes. Even though he wasn't yet six years old, Harry was showing an uncanny ability to remember lines and, encouraged by his teachers, often took the lead in student productions that included an ambitious attempt at *The Lion, The Witch and the Wardrobe*, a book he had first read with Prince Charles.

But Harry's finest moment on stage came at the Christmas concert when he gave a solo rendition of 'Good Christian Men Rejoice' in front of a packed audience that included his mother and father. He was beginning to love the limelight more and more as he discovered a natural ability to entertain others. He particularly loved entertaining crowds and revelled in the applause, whether it be from parents and friends during the annual school play or his fellow students breaking into guffaws of laughter in the playground. He was also prepared to perform anywhere, even acting the fool if he felt that would get him attention. During the celebrations to commemorate the Battle of Britain in 1990, six-year-old Harry attempted to dance the jitterbug with his two-year-old cousin Beatrice in the middle of a sombre prayer reading. The world's press again captured the moment on film, as well as his mother's somewhat bemused admonishment, gently informing her son to 'Put her down ... and sit still.'

If Harry was ever chastised like this in public by his mother, he would wreak revenge by taking her advice to behave himself to ludicrous lengths. At the VJ celebrations in 1995, he stood flanked by his parents and brother in a suit and tie with a look that said he was clearly bored out of his mind. At one point the cameras caught him making no attempt to conceal the fact he was yawning and looking at his watch. His mother raised her eyes skywards, shaking her head gently at this childish behaviour that was so often simply endearing.

Harry's love of acting also led to one of William's finest moments on stage. In 1994, while at school at Eton, William was offered the role of a tough American cop in a school production. Fearing an American accent might not sound too good coming from his cut-glass upper-class voice, William turned down the role. But Harry, on seeing the script, implored his brother to take the part pointing out that several scenes included the cop waving around a .357 Magnum pistol, and anything that included waving around a .357 Magnum would be fun in Harry's vivid and imaginative mind. Eventually William gave in and took the role. Photographs taken by the college perfectly capture the future King of England brandishing the huge pistol with a terrifying 'Ask yourself one question. Do I feel lucky? Well, do ya, punk?' expression.

CHAPTER SEVEN

In September 1992 Harry joined his brother as a boarder at Ludgrove School in Berkshire. By this time the world had read Andrew Morton's explosive *Diana: Her True Story*. Though not yet officially separated, Charles and Diana were already living apart. She continued to stay at Kensington Palace, leaving Charles to enjoy Highgrove at last with Camilla.

The school, just outside Bracknell and hidden among strawberry fields and farmers' meadows, was chosen originally for its privacy and easy policing by up to 20 royal protection officers. By the time Harry arrived he was considered a bright student who would embrace the school's curriculum, with its emphasis on sports and outdoor activities. The school, buried deep in the Berkshire countryside, also served another purpose. Both Harry and William were kept away from the tabloid newspapers that endlessly reported the so-called War of the Waleses in page after page of, often totally untrue, speculation.

On 9 December 1992, the Prime Minister John Major announced to a packed House of Commons that the Prince and Princess of Wales had decided to separate. The news was not unexpected, for several weeks now the tabloids had been running stories about the imminent separation as if it had already happened.

The day before, Princess Diana had driven down to Ludgrove School to tell William and Harry the news. The boys were ushered into headmaster Gerald Barber's office, where Diana sat with the head's wife Jane by her side. Diana, in a voice choking with emotion, patiently explained Mummy and Daddy would no longer be living together and how the new arrangements would affect them. William immediately burst into tears and asked his mother if she still loved Daddy. Diana herself started crying at that point and told him no matter what happened she would always love their father. She had used the same words on Charles himself when they had both agreed to the separation.

Harry, watching his mother cradle William, appeared unmoved by the tears. It was assumed he was, at the age of eight, too young to understand what was going on. In many ways he was used to his mother and father being apart, so there would be no dramatic change of life for him. Besides, Harry had started well at Ludgrove and was seen as a star pupil. Unlike most children of his age, he was keen to get back to class and buckle down to work.

But by Harry's tenth birthday, his schoolwork was beginning to show signs of slipping. While Harry had entered the school as an advanced student following glowing reports and exam results from his previous school, William, who had got over the tears of his parents' separation, was now fairing much better academically. Harry's teachers reported he was having difficulty in concentrating and did not seem much interested in lessons. It came as no surprise to Prince Charles when he later learned the school's attempts to keep the tabloids away from Harry and William had not been entirely successful. There were often a number of outside contractors working on the school grounds who would leave newspapers lying around. Even if William and Harry did not see them, their friends certainly did. Consequently some of the more sensational news headlines were further embellished by playground talk before they reached royal ears.

Both Prince Charles and Diana were sufficiently concerned to have one of the few amicable meetings since their *de facto* separation. They knew it was too obvious to blame Harry's problems on their split. Though this could be a factor, it was not considered significant; both Charles and Diana had friends in the modern age who had suffered separation and divorce and each had been told the same thing: children cope. The greater danger is when they are forced to watch their parents tear each other apart while trying to stay together for their sakes.

In many ways Charles and Diana's attitude towards each other was beginning to change for the better. To some extent Diana's press coverage, which had hitherto been almost fawning in its nature, was beginning to show a subtle change. Journalists, especially the highly influential columnists, were starting to question Diana's role in the break-up, in particular her collusion with Morton on his book, one of the few facts Britain's Royal Press Corps seemed to have got right that year. Until now it had been largely assumed that Charles was the villain of the marriage break-up, but, as a PR campaign launched by Charles's own staff began to kick in, some reporters were starting to question Diana's sainthood.

In Britain's biggest-selling newspaper, the *Sun*, columnist Richard Littlejohn, who enjoyed enormous support among the paper's 12 million readers, vowed never to mention the princess again, accusing her of hijacking every AIDS victim, sick baby, charity lunch, ribbon cutting, benefit concert or fundraising dinner for self-promotion and the chance of a photo op. Littlejohn, who once famously compared the Windsors to *The Godfather*'s Corleone family, went so far as to say Diana had signed her own death warrant the moment she began co-operating with Andrew Morton on his book and that she should now be happy with a house just off the M4 and access to her children. Like many a corrupt politician whose lies and sneers are lampooned by Littlejohn on a weekly basis, Diana's anger at his words could not entirely veil the fact that he had a point. In vain she protested to Charles that they had decided together she should maintain a high-profile public image for their children's sakes.

After the meeting with her husband about their separation, Diana drove down to Ludgrove for a chat with the teachers and Harry himself. Afterwards all sides seemed quite happy.

Harry's lack of interest in his schooling was more down to the natural reluctance of a child towards schooling than anything more serious. Diana's continued efforts to allow the boys to lead a normal life were encouraged by the school. Both Harry and William were seen to be benefiting from interaction with the public on their frequent outings with their mother, many of which involved visiting those who exist at the rougher end of the social scale.

Diana would go out of her way to show the boys the stark contrast between the royal life they enjoyed at home and the real world outside the palace walls. In 1993, during Ascot week, Diana organised a special day out for her boys. In the morning she took them to the Chelsea Harbour club in her new Audi convertible, amusing the boys by allowing them to lower the car roof. After a brisk game of tennis, Diana told her sons they would be making a very special visit later that evening to meet some nuns who ran a refuge night shelter for street people. When Harry asked what a 'street person' was, Diana explained that not everyone could afford a house and some people had no place to go at night. Perplexed, Harry asked if they couldn't stay at Kensington Palace. At 8 o'clock that evening, three cars pulled up outside the refuge, based in a modest house in Westminster. Diana and her sons were in the first car, the two other vehicles were police backup. The royal party was greeted inside by Sister Bridie Dowd, who led the boys through the main hall to meet the people who lodged there. While Diana mingled with the homeless men in one room, William and Harry were making their own introductions in another. William played chess with one of the men, using a chessboard made of cardboard for the first time in his life. Harry, meanwhile, was treated to a number of card tricks by one old hand, who insisted young Harry join in a quick hand of poker before he left.

Later that night, back at Kensington Palace, Diana and the boys spoke of the evening and the plight of the homeless. The event was unique in that it was never reported in the papers. Diana, with the help of her private secretary Patrick Jephson, had managed to keep the visit a complete secret from the press, proving the critics, who suggested everything she did was only for publicity purposes, completely wrong. Diana could easily have scored a spectacular PR coup by leaking the story to Fleet Street, which, considering the visit took place during Ascot week, would have made great show of the caring princess ignoring the champagne and smoked salmon of Ascot to take her boys to a homeless refuge. Diana wanted William and Harry to see the more brutal side of life, but she didn't want them to grow up thinking it was all bad outside the Palace walls. She would make sure they also got to meet everyday members of the public when they were out with her.

On one memorable occasion Diana took the boys to a nearby newsagents when she drove them out of school. The shopkeeper, Baresh Patel, served the royal trio without a second glance. To their astonishment, he simply had not recognised the world's most famous woman and her children. It was a moment to be savoured by Diana, and an incident that convinced her they could be taken for just a normal family. Even when he handed over the sweets and looked into Diana's face the penny still did not drop, despite the fact every newspaper he had handled that day carried on its front page a picture of the woman he was currently serving.

The boys continued to see a great deal of their mother towards the end of 1993. It was as if the princess, by now heavily involved in painful, yet top secret, divorce negotiations with Prince Charles, depended on them for the support she wasn't getting from her own family. A request made by her to her elder brother, the current Earl Spencer, to move back to the family home at Althorp had been rejected on the grounds that her presence would bring unwanted intrusion. The irony of this decision hurt Diana a great deal. The whole reason she wanted to move back to Althorp was to have the type of privacy she was no longer used to.

Diana and Charles were still seen in public but the rift between the two was ever growing. Indeed, the traditional staff Christmas party that year was the first time the estranged couple had seen each other in over a month. Despite the fact, Charles and Diana sat apart from each other throughout the festive celebration that was held at one of London's top restaurants, Simpson's in the Strand. One observer said Diana frequently 'glared' at Charles but conversation between the two was kept to a minimum. Over 60 staff tucked into the turkey lunch which was paid for by Charles and received gifts of crystal glass from both Waleses. Even though she put on a happy face for the staff, Diana was keen to leave the event as soon as she could. Further up the road in Kensington her two sons were enjoying their own Christmas party at Rolling Stone Bill Wyman's restaurant, Sticky Fingers, and Diana was keen to join in the fun.

Christmas that year was going to be very difficult for Diana and she knew it. Before attending the staff Christmas party, she had been told she was to lose one of her favourite bodyguards, Inspector Peter Brown. Even though Diana had told the Palace she wanted to cut down on her police protection, using minders only on official jobs and not using them at all in her private life, she was sad to see Inspector Brown leave, secretly she had been hoping he could be found a job within the Royal Protection Squad, but Scotland Yard were adamant he was going back to uniform.

Diana was also aware the annual Christmas cards she and Prince Charles always sent together were about to fall into the hands of the press. For the first time the two had issued separate cards. Prince Charles showed himself with his two sons comfortably sitting together on the lawn at Balmoral. It was a tender picture. The smiling young princes show none of the strain of their parents' separation as they rest fondly on their father. It was also the first time the public had seen any evidence that Charles could actually play the doting father. In stark contrast Diana's card, from which she had removed the royal crest for the Spencer family coat of arms, was far more formal and contrived. Diana, looking exceptionally beautiful, glances down at Prince William, her left hand nestling gently in front of him as William looks to camera. Harry, on her right, gazes towards the ceiling with the inquisitive look of a turn-of-the-century farmhand who has just seen his first barnstormer. The cards showed the public for the first time how wide the gulf between Charles and Diana had become, but Diana knew there was more trouble brewing.

The question of where the children would be spending Christmas had first been asked some months before. Diana desperately wanted to be with her children on Christmas Day, so had been invited to spend Christmas with the royals at Sandringham. But she wanted the boys at KP with her. The refusal Diana received came from the highest ranks of the royal family. Both the Queen and the Duke of Edinburgh were outraged at the suggestion that William and Harry would not be spending Christmas Day attending the annual service at church with them. Prince Charles sided with his parents all the way, even to the point of inviting Diana to spend the entire Christmas at Sandringham, something he certainly did not relish as he was hoping to spend time with his mistress. The Queen and the Duke were not too keen on that arrangement either; Diana was still considered slightly odd by both of them and they feared their traditional, family Christmas could be ruined by more scenes between Charles and Diana.

But they did not bargain for Diana's response. Realising she would not be able to beat the senior royals on this one she refused to spend any more time at Sandringham than she had to, and even snubbed the offer to dine with the royals at Christmas lunch, telling Prince Charles she would be with her boys and that he could stuff his turkey. Eventually she stayed for less than 24 hours at Sandringham, before flying off the New York to spend Christmas with friends. Later she admitted to crying her way through that lonely Christmas.

Again, it is very hard not to sympathise with Diana; loving her children as much as she did it must have been torture to leave them, but the increasingly bitter, and petty, arguments that seemed to follow the separation were beginning to affect the children. It was just after Christmas that the strain finally got to young Harry. Only a couple of months past his ninth birthday, he read in the papers how his mother had flown to America to avoid being home alone in London.

Diana had spent New Year with her best friend Lucia Flecha de Lima, the wife of the Brazilian Ambassador to America. On New Year's Day, feeling tired and lonely, she rang Sandringham to speak to William and Harry and wish them a Happy New Year. The switchboard operator at Sandringham did not know where Charles or the children were, so Diana asked to be put through to the Queen. Her Majesty, somewhat surprised to discover Diana did not know the whereabouts of her own family, reminded her that Charles, William and Harry were staying with friends at Anmer Hall, just up the road from Sandringham. Diana apologised, explained she had forgotten and began to say goodbye. The Queen, possibly sensing the loneliness Diana must be feeling so far from her children, asked her if everything was all right. Diana took the chance to confide in the Queen, blurting out she was dreadfully lonely and missing her children very badly. The two women then had a 20-minute conversation, during which the Queen assured Diana the children were missing her too. The Queen knew this to be a fact, as a sad note had entered the holiday when, on Monday, 27 December, Harry went for a long walk alone around the Sandringham estate. One worker who saw the prince's solitary walk claimed the young prince was 'crying his eyes out'.

Despite her own marital problems, Diana continued to go out of her way to show both William and Harry the real world. During a trip to Wales she insisted the royal party forsake the traditional royal plane or limo and take the train. Armed with a copy of *The Economist*, the voice of England's intellectual right wing and hardly her usual reading matter, she boarded a train at Paddington with her two sons, telling waiting reporters they were heading off for a 'bit of culture'.

Harry, in particular, loved the train and stood in the corridor throughout the journey with his head out of the window. At one point he exclaimed, 'There's a train coming,' with great excitement and much to the annoyance of his minder, who tentatively pointed out it may be a good idea for Harry to get his head back in. Harry, of course, did not, he shrieked as the other train roared by and laughed at both the policeman's and his mother's concerns. Following his window scare Harry then thought it would be fun to spark a major security alert by locking himself in the train toilet. He bolted the door as a prank and it was only his mother's irate hammering and threats on the door that eventually forced the young prince to open up only to be unceremoniously pulled out and marched back to his seat by Diana.

But more and more Harry was becoming protective towards his mother. He was old enough to know all was not going well between her and his father and could see the strain on his mother's face each time she had to hand them back at the end of the frequent visits. Once, Harry launched himself at a press photographer at London's Dominion theatre. The boys were again with their mother to see a production of the hit play

Grease. Unfortunately, though the trip was a private event, Diana and the boys arrived on the same night three or four members of the notorious paparazzi were staking out the theatre, following a tip-off that a well-known celebrity would be inside with a woman other than his wife.

On seeing Diana and her two sons the paparazzi reaction was predictable. Flashguns were fired as a harassed-looking Diana ordered her detectives to 'Get rid of them'. Scuffles then broke out between the snappers and the police during which Harry was clearly heard to use the word 'tossers'. It is unlikely he was referring to the policemen. His comment was probably influenced by an incident earlier that week when his mother had been ambushed by a press photographer as she drove to Highgrove on the M4. She uttered some very choice curses …

The family had also recently seen a trip to watch the fireworks at Tetbury ruined by press intrusion. Princess Diana and her children were forced to flee to a waiting car when it was realised there were more camera flashes filling the air with bright light than there were fireworks.

But, more and more, Harry was beginning to show signs of being oblivious to danger. At Windsor Castle he had recently been spotted firing a shotgun from the sunroof of an estate car, standing up on the passenger seat like a modern day Rooster Cogburn and letting the rabbit population of the castle have it with both barrels. Harry was said to be trying to better his elder brother, who had recently been photographed in a combat jacket while hunting rabbits on the Queen's estate at Balmoral. The resulting pictures were splashed across the tabloids the following day, with headlines such as HARRY'S GAME, and copy that asked whether Harry was safe standing on the passenger seat of a moving car and firing a shotgun at passing rabbits. It wasn't that serious, but it was a taste of things to come.

In September 1995, as Harry turned eleven, his life changed again when his elder brother left Ludgrove for Eton College and for the first time in his young life Harry found himself alone. The daunting prospect of getting through the next two years at Ludgrove without the support of his elder brother was further compounded that weekend when Princess Diana made an unexpected visit to see him.

After watching the young prince play football, Diana, who had sat alone throughout the match, took Harry for a short walk. Leaning against the fence of a field, as cows mooed just yards away, Diana informed her son she had given an exclusive interview to the BBC that was to be screened the following week. She told Harry first and the following day she drove to Eton to tell William. The response from both of them was the same. Harry, like his brother the following day, could only groan on hearing the news, a groan that was echoed throughout the royal family as everyone asked the same question: 'Oh Lord ... What is she up to?'

They had to wait a week to find out when, along with half the population of Great Britain, the royal family tuned their TV sets to the BBC and watched the most intimate interview ever given by a senior member of Britain's monarchy, as Diana opened her heart to what she still saw as her public. (Everyone that is except the Queen and Duke of Edinburgh, who chose to watch *Cracker* on the other side instead.) Dressed almost provocatively in a black suit, with dark eye shadow, Diana dropped bombshell after bombshell into her husband's lap. She spoke of his infidelity with Camilla, and her infidelity with Hewitt. When she was in the wrong it was only because others had made it appear that way, she seemed to be saying.

It was shameless, it was manipulative ... it was a staggering success. Diana, the first royal in history to use the media for her own benefits to such a great extent, was effectively letting the family know just how much damage she could inflict on them, like a country dropping the nuclear bomb before the peace negotiations get under way. Diana's appearance on *Panorama* would one day be seen for what it was, the most public divorce demand in history.

Her ploy worked. The following day the Queen's private secretary got in touch with Prince Charles and informed him that Her Majesty would like the divorce arrangements straightened out and finalised now. Charles, still reeling from the body-blow Diana had served up with her TV appearance, knew an order when he heard one. He instructed his lawyers to sort the divorce out even if it meant giving in to all of Diana's demands. The lawyers said it could be expensive. Charles replied it already was.

Earlier, in 1993, Harry had joined the ranks of working royals when he accompanied his mother on a short trip to Germany to visit one of the army regiments with whom she was involved. Still fascinated by everything military, nine-year-old Harry jumped at the chance of meeting the soldiers of the

Light Dragoons Regiment. During what at first appeared an innocent conversation with his mother on the plane home Harry was surprised when Diana asked him how he would feel if he had to take William's place and be the next king.

Harry was perplexed, even confused by the question. Why had his mother asked it? Diana looked away and, making light of the moment, she tried to turn it into a joke but observers on the plane said both the prince and his mother lapsed into silence. After a few moments Harry blurted out, 'I shall be King Harry … I shall do all the work.' Diana told him to 'ssssshh'.

CHAPTER EIGHT

During the Easter holidays of 1993, when Harry was nine years old, a welcome breath of fresh air entered his life, in the shape of a new nanny: a person he would eventually end up loving very deeply, but initially someone he took little notice of. Tiggy Legge-Bourke was the young woman that Prince Charles had chosen to help care for his sons when they were staying with him. She was to become a friend to both of them, more of a big sister than an au pair, and someone they could both talk to and confide in. Despite some hints in the press about Charles's relationship with the vivacious and attractive Tiggy, she shrugged off the more blatant inaccuracies and eventually became almost a part of the family, someone who cared for the boys with genuine warmth and love.

Diana was beside herself with rage that Tiggy should

suddenly be installed as a surrogate mother and demanded of Charles to know all of Tiggy's duties. The princess even went so far as to phone Tiggy and tell her in no uncertain terms, 'I'm the boys' mother, thank you very much.' Ignoring Diana's criticism and barbed comments that questioned her own schooling, Tiggy eventually became a major force in the lives of both boys. With Tiggy beside them, the boys experienced an endless summer of exciting games where there always seemed to be something new. Swimming, horse riding, skateboarding, rabbit shooting and cycling were all activities the indefatigable Tiggy led them on, always explaining, showing them how to handle a gun or a skateboard with equal skill. Both boys were amazed at how versatile and exhaustive Tiggy's talents were. In some ways her sporting prowess and zest for life were very similar to their mother's.

Officially, Tiggy, who in 1993 was 30 years old, was hired as an assistant to Charles's private secretary, Commander Richard Aylard. In reality, it was very rare that she went anywhere near the office. There seemed to be no need for her to be involved in official work either, an obvious discrepancy in her job title that gave Diana ammunition to claim Tiggy was no more than an au pair. She was paid £20,000 a year, slightly above average for an academically qualified nanny in London.

Within a few months of arriving at Highgrove Tiggy had become best friend to both boys, but it was Harry who became most attached to her, treating her equally as his best friend and main rival, someone who could take William's place in Harry's ever-competitive world. Harry and Tiggy embarked on an almost never-ending round of horse races and frantic skateboarding with each of them trying to outdo the other. After falling off the skateboard one time too often, Tiggy would lie on the ground laughing, while Harry implored her to get up and start again.

Tiggy, whose real name is Alexandra, was the quintessential upper-class girl. She was raised in the Welsh mountains on her parents' family estate, Glanusk Park, which occupies 6,000 acres around Crickhowell, one of the most beautiful areas in Wales. She had first been educated at St David's Convent in Brecon, South Wales, an independent Roman Catholic School of 150 pupils run by the Ursuline order of nuns. She then moved to the Manor House in Durnford, an elite prep school of only 50 girls, owned by Lady Tyron, the mother-in-law of Charles's old friend Lady 'Kanga' Tyron.

At the age of 13, Tiggy moved to Heathfield, Ascot in Berkshire, one of Britain's top girls' boarding schools, where she enjoyed herself among the jolly hockey sticks and debutante humour of the refined students. She excelled at netball and tennis, though she was not deemed particularly bright academically. Though extremely popular with fellow pupils and ending her schooling with glowing reports, she attained only four 'o'levels. The lack of academic achievement did not worry Tiggy; she already knew her personality was a far greater asset than her brain.

Ironically Tiggy completed her education by attending the same exclusive Swiss finishing school as Princess Diana near Gstaad. It was here that Tiggy played the sports and games that were to make her so popular with William and Harry. Not only was she extremely capable at tennis, lacrosse, netball and fencing, she also shared both boys' love of camping. Swimming, riding, hunting, stalking, fishing and skiing were all enjoyed by the trio on the royal estates of Balmoral and Sandringham. For Harry, life with Tiggy was one long holiday that he hoped would never end.

Despite Diana's continued misgivings, she had to admit that Tiggy's credentials for looking after the young princes were impeccable. Before being hired for the job, Tiggy had spent time training to look after young people. In 1985, after having attended a Montessori nursery-teaching course in London, she opened her own nursery in Battersea, South London. It was named 'Mrs Tiggiwinkle' after the famous hedgehog character of Beatrix Potter's children's books, which she loved, and the film of which she watched with both Harry and William. (The video was borrowed from the Queen's personal video library at Windsor Castle along with *Yellow Submarine*.)

Tiggy's nursery was a great success. She discovered she had a natural affinity with children and her school for toddlers became very popular. Three years later, however, Tiggy's school got into financial difficulties and, much to her intense disappointment, Mrs Tiggiwinkle closed down.

Diana's repeated concerns to friends and off-the-record quotes to favoured journalists about Tiggy's influence over Prince Charles were met with scorn by the press. They believed Tiggy was hired genuinely for the boys' sakes, tactfully pointing out, as only the British press can, that Tiggy was not exactly a fashion icon. On this issue they did, at least, have a point. Tiggy was as happy wearing jeans, wellington boots and a tee shirt and sweater all day, as dressing up in an expensive outfit and high-heeled shoes. And, the biggest crime in the tabloid press's minds, she wore little make-up.

Within weeks of taking the job, however, Tiggy had earned the respect of both William and Harry in her own, indomitable fashion. Prince Charles had organised a day hunting and shooting rabbits on the Sandringham estate. Both William and Harry were amazed at Tiggy's ability with a gun. Harry was particularly impressed with a direct hit fired from the hip.

William, Harry and Tiggy became a familiar trio that seemed forever laughing. Sometimes they would be joined by Prince Charles and they began to take on the appearance of a family, something which particularly irked an angry Diana, who was inclined to interpret it as an elaborate conspiracy to steal her children's love.

As Harry grew older, he would try even harder to compete with Tiggy. He was aware he was being left behind in the growing stakes, especially as his elder brother William was nearly Tiggy's equal in height and certainly in strength. Consequently Harry became more aggressive in their games, once even catching Tiggy full in the face with a football. It led to one of their few disagreements and ended with Harry storming off in anger – a move that earned him a severe reprimand from his brother.

The only other row the three ever had involved Tiggy's absolute refusal to give up smoking. William despaired of Tiggy's habit, especially as he had discussed the whole issue of cancer at great length with his mother following a death in the family of a school friend. Harry, though not as outspoken as

William on the smoking issue, ridiculed Tiggy about having to stand outside when she smoked because of Prince Charles's refusal to allow it in the house.

When the trio were at Highgrove or Balmoral William would usually take the initiative in planning the days together, giving himself the opportunity to test his growing strength and leadership qualities at her and Harry's expense. In many ways the boys were developing their characters under Tiggy's guidance. When they first met Tiggy, William was ten and Harry eight. Of the two boys, Harry was the quieter one. William, nicknamed Terrible Wills by Highgrove staff, never spoke if it was possible to shout. Yet both boys changed after they met Tiggy. Harry became the loud one, as he showed off to the woman he now considered an older sister. They would often have mock fights together in their bedrooms or a lounge, when they would grapple on the sofa before falling sprawled out on to the floor, screaming with laughter, continuing to tussle with each other. It was not unusual during these bouts for William and Harry to team up against poor Tiggy, launching pre-arranged assaults the moment the commercial break came during an evening's viewing in front of the TV.

But pillow fights were their favourite, occasionally using the scatter cushions on the sofa. They would hurl the missiles at each other in the opulent surroundings of Balmoral Castle or Sandringham estate, the boys trying to hit Tiggy full in the face. Each success was greeted with a scream of delight, and Tiggy would throw a pillow back at them, their squeals of fun resounding through whichever palace they found themselves in. This was another great attraction to the boys; Tiggy was no shrinking violet and was quite capable of taking care of herself with the two of them. Within six months of Tiggy's arrival, both William and Harry were having the time of their lives.

Despite her wish for them to be happy, this was also the cause of much frustration for their mother. Diana was becoming increasingly isolated in London and had craved the company of her sons ever since the official announcement of her separation. Any threat Diana felt from Tiggy was of her own making. The reality was exactly what Charles had planned when he had first hired a new nanny. Tiggy had a steadying influence on both William and Harry, for she channelled her enthusiasm and exuberant spirit into a more outdoor, energetic life that took their minds away from their parents' marital problems.

Harry, in particular, adored Tiggy. He was probably still too young to understand that he had a crush on her. Although she was considered to be nothing more than an au pair by his mother, she was a woman who made Harry want to be bigger and better, and his attempts to gain her approval were tireless.

But Tiggy had two charges and, despite Harry constantly being by her side, she tried to spend some time alone with William. Unfortunately, this made Harry jealous, especially when William began to confide in Tiggy the type of thoughts he had thus far only told Harry. Thoughts such as how, despite his mother and father's efforts, he knew everything about their marriage's collapse, as he had since he was a child and he would push paper tissues under the bathroom door to his mother, locked in and weeping, inside.

Prince Charles was more than happy that William should confide in Tiggy, even if he could see Harry's growing resentment at what he considered being left out. To Charles, the fact William had found a soulmate was an added bonus of Tiggy's employment. He appreciated how his sons and Tiggy enjoyed their lives together, and watched with satisfaction how casually they lay around the TV room watching a video or, more than likely, playing football in the yard at Highgrove.

Tiggy had been asked by Charles to make sure Harry and William enjoyed themselves, and to his mind her job was a wonderful success. But Charles also warned Tiggy not to spoil them. And he also told her that if any problems arose he was to be informed immediately. Charles had always felt guilty that his relationship with Diana had ended in tears and trauma, and he was determined to endeavour to shield the boys from the effects of the marriage break-up. To Charles, William and Harry and their upbringing was of paramount importance, far more important than his own happiness. For Charles knew only too well how unhappy and miserable a young boy can feel when brought up in an environment where there was little or no love and affection. To some extent Charles had always loved the fact that Diana showed him how to feel compassion, how to hold his sons and give them love. He owed her for that and he knew it.

With this in mind, at the start of Tiggy's employment Charles took her to one side and explained how jealous Diana could get if she thought another person was stealing her children's feelings. Therefore, Charles asked her to, hold back just a bit. He had no need to fear because Tiggy had a wise head on her shoulders. She did not spoil the boys or show them any special signs of affection when others were around. But, as the relationships progressed Tiggy found herself genuinely caring about William and Harry. She discovered there was no need to take charge of the boys, that even at such a young age they were showing a perceptive awareness of their world. Thus decisions between the three, ranging from what game they would play that day to how many sweets one should be allowed to eat between meals, were reached by democratic means.

Harry loved his time with Tiggy, especially the outdoor activities, but William was becoming increasingly protective towards his mother. He could not shake off the doubt that he was, in some way, being disloyal to his mother by wanting to be with the happy, carefree Tiggy. William was also acutely aware Diana was increasingly looking on Tiggy as yet another 'plant' by the Palace, who she suspected, wrongly, of plotting against her. Diana already knew she could not count on Prince Charles's private secretary Commander Aylard, who was currently involved in a dramatic PR campaign to boost his master's public image. And Diana remained deeply suspicious of the Queen's press secretary Charles Anson, the man who had famously revealed, 'The knives are out for Fergie at the Palace.' Fuelled by stories in the tabloids, the princess became convinced that Fergie's castigation and exile by the Palace was a preliminary for the main bout – her own demise.

Harry too was painfully aware of his mother's suspicion of Tiggy Legge-Bourke, seeing her as a threat to her own role as a mother and regarding anything Tiggy did for the boys with anger and wariness. Diana would tell friends Tiggy was gaining too great an influence over her sons, but any sympathy for Diana's complaints would be negated when the princess would launch into a series of fantasy scenarios that still included references to the royal family and MI5 being involved in a conspiracy to deprive her of her children's love.

When Tiggy was first employed by Prince Charles, and Diana had ordered her private secretary to write to the prince and demand to know exactly what Tiggy's involvement with the boys would be, Diana never received what she felt to be a satisfactory answer. This caused Diana to become increasingly nasty and spiteful in her references to Tiggy, who she would describe to anyone who would listen as 'that woman who looks like a man'.

But, during Christmas 1995, Diana went too far, and an incident took place which revealed that the world's best-loved princess could also be a vindictive and vitriolic woman who was capable of causing great pain to others. It happened at the staff Christmas party. Princess Diana had somehow managed to contrive a ludicrous, and entirely incorrect, story that Tiggy had recently had an abortion. The father of the terminated baby was not named in Diana's fantasy, but anyone who heard her tell the story could be left in no doubt that Charles himself was the prime suspect. As the combined offices of Charles and Diana enjoyed a Christmas spread, Diana crept up behind Tiggy and whispered, 'So sorry to hear about the baby' in her ear.

Tiggy's reaction, like anybody's, was predictable and, possibly, what Diana wanted. The woman who had done no more wrong than befriend Diana's children collapsed sobbing at the malicious, false and wounding remark while a triumphant Diana left the room grinning from ear to ear. Diana's private secretary, Patrick Jephson, brought up the rear. He had already been briefed on Diana's triumph by the princess herself and now followed his boss with his head in his hands, knowing she had gone too far. Indeed Jephson, possibly fearing legal retribution against Diana, asked, 'Ma'am ... have you any evidence?'

'I don't need evidence, I know ...' replied Diana, with a triumphant glint in her eye.

'Oh Jesus Christ,' replied Jephson, still holding his head in anguish.

The ugliness of the incident is perhaps best summed up by Jephson's response. Living in the real world, increasingly unlike his boss, Jephson knew she would not be allowed to get away with what she had just said, and it was no surprise when a legal letter arrived from Tiggy's lawyers. Diana was forced to undertake a guarantee she would not repeat the clearly untrue remarks. Prince Charles pacified Tiggy by explaining Diana had been under tremendous pressure recently and the matter, though already resolved through legal channels, was laid to rest.

The incident shows, however, how far Diana was prepared to go in her campaign against Tiggy. Ignoring the obvious love her children had for their nanny, Diana continued to believe she had chalked up a minor victory with her awful remarks, but she could not have been more wrong. After that Christmas party, Diana's staff began to jump ship like rats, leaving a bewildered and no longer exultant, Diana asking, 'What have I done wrong now?'

Diana had also believed that, when Harry was with Tiggy, he seemed to forget about her. Her concerns were, of course, without foundation. Harry, oblivious to his mother's growing paranoia, was simply enjoying the company of a woman he loved to be with; in no way did Tiggy ever replace any aspect of Diana's relationship with Harry. But Diana continued to see plots and conspiracies everywhere and the simplest thing could set her off again. During the autumn half-term holidays in 1993, Harry was with his father at Balmoral. Diana, who was due to fly to Brussels to help promote the European Year of the Elderly, was upset when Harry, out playing football with Tiggy, had refused to take a last-minute call she made from the airport. Diana had already been upset by a set of pictures in that day's papers that showed just how close Harry and Tiggy had become as they frolicked by the side of the River Dee.

A long, tearful conversation with Prince Charles convinced Diana her concerns were unfounded. Charles pointed out that there may well have been schoolboy problems that Harry and William did not wish to discuss with either of their parents. Having an adult who they treated as an equal was a perfect valve for those confusing concerns that the children of separated parents always have. Harry too began seeking Tiggy's advice and, during the next five years, a remarkable relationship developed between both boys and Tiggy, which would prove invaluable when the moment came for real comfort, love and support to be distributed in huge quantities.

CHAPTER NINE

After two years of bickering and argument, media battles and tantrums, an agreement was finally hammered out over the royal divorce. The final document relating to both sides' demands was handed to the Queen for her approval, an action that did not sit well with Diana's camp, who were heard to mutter, 'Exactly who is divorcing who here?'

Diana was to receive an alimony lump sum of around £8 million, to be paid in instalments, and she would be allowed to keep her apartments at Kensington Palace. The money was irrelevant, as Diana was already fabulously wealthy from a trust her father had set up for her as a child. She had also received many priceless gifts during her marriage, and, though technically they belonged to the state, nobody fancied going to court to prove it.

The most controversial part of the agreement concerned Diana's role once she was outside the royal family. She would have to give up her royal title, an announcement that was met with much anger from a still adoring public, and be known henceforth as Diana, Princess of Wales. Though she would remain a princess, the removal of Diana's title proved absolute victory for the Queen, who had now effectively banished both her daughters-in-law from the royal family.

The question of custody had never arisen during any of the negotiations. Under British constitutional law the boys, as heirs to the throne, would automatically have stayed with their father. But Charles had told Diana from the start of their separation that she would always have equal custody of the children no matter what happened elsewhere in the negotiations. Diana was genuinely thankful to Charles for this, a small gesture that allowed her an even hand on the roulette table that they were both facing. Charles was making it clear that, no matter how messy things got, he would never use the children against Diana.

Charles and Diana filed for divorce on 15 July 1996. They were granted a decree nisi on 28 August, just two weeks short of Harry's twelfth birthday. Diana received the news that the agreement had been reached while sitting in a car-park on her own just outside Eton. After she hung up she put her mobile phone down on the passenger seat and wept.

Harry's relationship with his mother now entered a new phase. He was old enough to question certain aspects of his own life, such as the privileges of royalty. 'How do I get Cup Final tickets?' was one of the more innocent questions Harry asked his mother during a summer afternoon shopping spree in London's West End.

On 9 March 1997 Charles and Diana, accompanied by William and Harry, arrived at St George's Chapel in Windsor. The event was William's confirmation, but public and press interest was mainly on the Prince and Princess of Wales. For the first time in years they seemed relaxed together. Charles took Diana's arm and whispered something in her ear as they walked through the castle gates, and she giggled. In a later nostalgic discussion with the castle staff, Diana reminded Charles how they had been at Windsor the weekend Harry was born. To both of them it all seemed so long ago.

The family was finally relaxed together after years of turmoil, argument and suspicion. After William's confirmation they enjoyed tea with the castle chaplain. Neither Diana nor Charles were in any rush to leave. Each was enjoying the company of the other as they caught up on gossip, while their sons regaled them with tales from school. William spoke of a sudden craving for wine gums and Diana revealed how she could never eat the black ones. Prince Charles confessed he had never had a wine gum, but had enjoyed a chewy sweet called a 'blackjack' which he would buy from the school tuck shop by the ton, as you could purchase eight for an old penny.

Charles and Harry spoke excitedly of a trip to Aldershot army town they were both preparing for, Harry beside himself with excitement that his father was taking him to the very home of the British army. Eye witnesses say they were just like any normal family in the formal surroundings of Windsor

Castle. 'You would never believe they were separated,' said one man, who had watched Charles and Diana talking with the children, 'they were so happy, so relaxed together.' It was an observation made by cynical press photographers outside who told their newsdesks in an excited babble, 'It's just like the old days,' as they remembered the time when the world was convinced that this was the love story of the century.

Thus Charles and Diana were able to put the bitter years behind them and embark on a new life with mutual respect. The days of fighting were over, they had both hurt and been hurt, both had wounds that would never heal, the scars were too deep. But the war and the battles were over and both had come through relatively unscathed. Though Diana still loved Charles she had come to terms with losing him. And Charles was aware, even though Diana had made some serious mistakes over the past two years, that she was now starting to make judgements based on experience, and was also beginning to discover some personal happiness in her love life.

Photographs printed the following day showed just how close the family had come despite the years of painful, and petty, arguments. The pictures clearly showed a family reconciled, two parents who had come to terms with their divorce and two loving children. Some papers, believing the glowing reports their photographers had hastily filed, even speculated on the possibility of Charles and Diana getting back together. Just six months before her tragic death they had finally become what Diana had always wanted them to be ... a happy family. What nobody could have dreamt at the time was that Prince William's confirmation at Windsor Castle on that cold March day was the last time Harry was ever to be seen in public with both his parents.

On 1 July 1997, Princess Diana was 36. Instinctively knowing his mother would be depressed spending her birthday at home, Harry rang her from school and sang 'Happy Birthday' down the phone. It was a gesture that had Diana in floods of tears. After telling Harry through choked tears she loved him very dearly she spoke excitedly of their forthcoming holiday together.

Diana had received an invitation from Harrods boss Mohammed Fayed to spend some time at his magnificent seaside estate at St Tropez in the South of France. Fayed had also promised to supply a yacht for Diana and her children's use. She promised Harry that Fayed's estate was big enough to offer them the privacy the family so craved on holiday together. After getting Harry's approval, Diana called William and received the news he too was keen on the South of France. Indeed William had said the same thing as Harry, 'Whatever you want, Mum ...'

And so Diana called Fayed to accept the invitation.

CHAPTER TEN

News that Diana and her boys were spending a vacation with Fayed was not greeted with enthusiasm in England. The newspapers openly questioned her judgement about spending time with Britain's most controversial tycoon, a man who had been branded a 'liar' and 'guilty of deception on a grand scale' by the Government. Successive Home Secretaries from both Conservative and Labour Governments had steadfastly refused to give the Egyptian-born Fayed a British passport, and his attempts to corrupt parliament during the 'cash for questions' scandal were the final nail in the Conservative Government's coffin, ensuring that he will never get what he craves – British citizenship.

It would be very hard to find a more unsuitable escort or host for a member of Britain's royal family. Indeed, it is hard not to agree with cynical reporters who suggested Diana's motive for accepting the holiday had more to do with sticking her two fingers up at the Establishment that she still believed was out to get her. What better way to hurt them than be entertained by the number one *persona non grata* on their list?

As was expected, Diana's arrival in St Tropez was met with derision by the British press, who, like many of their readers, genuinely felt Diana had made a big mistake. Today, close friends point out even Diana's best friend and confidante, Rosa Monckton, wife of the editor of the *Sunday Telegraph*, begged her not to accept the invitation. Other friends pointed out that the princess and her boys could hardly expect a private holiday in the South of France, home to the French paparazzi who, along with their Italian colleagues, were among the most ruthless photographers in the world. Even the British paparazzi, who had long ruled the roost when it came to pictures of Princess Diana, were not too keen on taking on their French counterparts. As photographer Glenn Harvey put it, 'No matter what anyone ever says about the British paps, we always respected Diana. To us she was a member of our royal family. With the French and the Italians there was no such respect. In some ways they even felt they were getting one over on England by beating us to the scoops. It's a brave snapper who takes those guys on ...'

The following day, the *News of the World* carried the banner headline 'DI AND SLEAZE ROW TYCOON'. Not to be outdone, the paper's main rival, the *Sunday Mirror*, accused Diana of freeloading with the headline 'DI'S FREEBIE'. It was the worst tabloid coverage Diana had ever had and something that caused her concern as she unpacked in St Tropez. Had she made a mistake?

The holiday was not a success. Despite Mohammed Fayed claiming he gave the young princes the 'best holiday of their lives' both William and Harry were far too aware that, yet again, certain people may be using their mother for publicity purposes. To the boys it was just a re-run of the Hewitt affair. Just another man bearing gifts and using them to get close to their mother. Even the arrival of Dodi Fayed, ordered to the villa by his father despite the fact he was staying in Paris with his current girlfriend, was seen by Harry and William as extremely suspicious.

Dodi Fayed was 41 years old and had spent his whole life never bothering to live up to the expectations people had of him. The only thing Dodi showed any aptitude for was spending his father's money. He brought fast cars and celebrity girlfriends at an alarming rate and enjoyed a playboy lifestyle that was almost obscene in its pointlessness. He had been married once, for eight months to the model Suzanne Gregard, but not happily, and he later complained that the experience had put him off marriage for life. Finding consolation in a string of beautiful girlfriends, including the actress Brooke Shields, Dodi seemed content to skim across the surface of life buying friends and friendship with a generosity that far outstripped his not exactly meagre allowance. Dodi had sealed his love for his latest girlfriend, the model Kelly Fisher, with a cheque for $200,000 – unfortunately for the Californian lovely, it bounced.

He liked to call himself a film producer, but the title holds no real meaning in the film world. David Puttnam and Sydney Pollack are film producers. Comparing the efforts of Dodi to them is like comparing Victoria Beckham to Judy Garland or Billie Holiday. In reality, Dodi was an executive producer: the type of person so beloved of Hollywood filmmakers because they stump up the cash for the movies but have no say in any part of the production. In that summer of 1997, Dodi's claim to fame was putting up most of the cash for an English film called *Chariots of Fire*, 16 years before. The movie went on to scoop the Oscar for best picture in 1982, despite American film executives claiming 'this film will do nothing in the States'. It was a lucky break for Dodi, who hadn't actually bothered to read the script, preferring instead to wine and dine David Puttnam et al and bask in the glory of finally producing a hit movie. It was a success that was never repeated.

Chariots of Fire went on to be an unexpected hit in America, and gave Dodi an air of respectability within the film world. In reality he was considered to be just another rich Arab with far too much money and nothing to do with it by the close-knit Hollywood community who, though they were happy to take his investment, certainly never put him anywhere near any lists prefaced 'A'. To return to the *Godfather* movies simile, Dodi was similar to Fredo Corleone, sent off to California to run some Mickey Mouse Film Company but never allowed anywhere near the family business.

For their mother's sake, both William and Harry made a determined effort to enjoy themselves, despite their own misgivings about Fayed's motives. Daily they frolicked in the warm waters of the Mediterranean, despite the ever-growing number of press photographers they had been promised wouldn't be able to get near them. Both the boys felt they were being used. For a private holiday this was one of the most public they had ever been on. Every day paparazzi photographers lined up with the gleeful enthusiasm of heavily armed soldiers in a trench who are told the enemy are coming at them without any weapons. It is ironic that the most private of all holidays eventually became the most public. Fayed's security was virtually non-existent and seemed to consist of a solitary speedboat pointing out to the photographers where the yacht was and what time the princess and her boys would be boarding.

At times, when they forgot the press, the boys did enjoy themselves. They both donned lifejackets with their mum and jet-skied in front of what by now appeared to be the world's entire population of press photographers. They were also treated to a late-night disco, which had been rented out by Dodi and sprinkled with a number of nubile young girls press-ganged from the beaches of St Tropez that day. The holiday could have been a success for the boys had they not realised very early on that everything they did was being passed on by someone to the world's press.

The situation wasn't exactly helped by Mohammed Fayed basking in the reflected glory of having Diana as his holiday companion and contriving a romance between Dodi and Diana. It came as no surprise to the boys when, following first reports of the romance, Dodi told Harrods spokesman, Michael Cole: 'I'll never have another girlfriend.' This nugget of 'private conversation' was immediately released to an obliging press who, armed with several other such gems, usually supplied by Fayed's own people, began to concoct the inevitable headlines despite the fact Diana herself had insisted she had no intention of marrying anyone in the foreseeable future.

Back in England, the Queen phoned Prince Charles as page after page of tabloid newspaper was filled with photographers of William, Harry and Diana frolicking in the Mediterranean. Charles insisted Diana would not have known the photographers were there, that she positively hated this type of media coverage. The Queen could only be suspcious as she looked at the photographs and, with a practised eye, noticed they were hardly the usual, long-lens, grainy, hardly identifiable images the paparazzi produced.

Harry became increasingly frustrated as the holiday went on. It seemed that everything they did was being carried out in the full glare of the world's media. He had known press harassment before, of course; three years earlier in southern Spain he had told a press photographer to 'piss off' after the snapper got too close on the beach, but in St Tropez nobody seemed to be doing anything to prevent the press getting as close as they wanted to. Fayed insisted his bodyguards riding in speedboats around the yacht would keep the press away, but both Harry and William could see that this was not happening. Both the boys were veterans of countless Mediterranean cruises with their father around the Greek Islands and knew damn well the easiest way to avoid the gathering press was to lift anchor and head out to sea.

Harry's frustrations eventually led to an incident that could have marred the holiday. During a childish argument between Harry and Omar Fayed, Mohammed Fayed's youngest son, the two boys squared up to each other on the yacht. Omar insisted that Harry stop arguing with him and demanded his own way. Harry reacted as he was increasingly prone to those days. 'Yes!' said one bodyguard. 'Prince Harry kicked his ass.'

On the last day of the holiday, Harry packed his own suitcase in the room he had shared with his brother William. Ultimately the holiday had been a disappointment. Harry was tired of the constant press intrusion, even though, unlike his brother, he bore no ill-feeling towards the photographers. And he disliked the fawning attentions his mother had received from Dodi Fayed. Like William, Harry was well aware his mother had struck up a personal relationship with a doctor called Hasnat Khan, back in London, and felt there were some dangerous adult games being played here of which he was wary. Closing his suitcase on the double bed, Harry stared wistfully out of the window across the perfect and seemingly untouched blue of the Mediterranean sea.

The holiday was over.

CHAPTER ELEVEN

The British public had been rather indifferent to Prince Harry. To them he was the 'cute one', adored almost as the runt of the litter. It wasn't until his mother's funeral, a day on which the world seemed to stand still, that he broke everyone's hearts with his 'Mummy' card, placed on the front of the coffin.

It would be too simple and obvious to blame Harry's later misdemeanours on his mother's death. It would also be wrong. So much has been said and written about Diana's death that the informed reader can reach his or her own conclusions on how a 12-year-old boy would cope with the unspeakable horror of his mother's death. However, there was a significant enough period of time between the tragic events of Paris, in August 1997, and Harry's front page appearance in the *News of the World*, to suggest that Harry's behaviour had more to do with his natural rebelliousness than Diana's death.

After Diana's funeral, Harry, despite suffering unimaginable grief alongside his brother, William, sought solace in the company of the only other woman he truly loved, Tiggy Legge-Bourke. Prince Charles had arranged for the boys to be excused school and took them back to Highgrove. Tiggy had also been invited.

Still too upset to face anyone, Harry spent a week with Tiggy, poring over thousands and thousands of condolences sent from around the world. Like a lot of people who have suffered a loss, Harry found some comfort in the messages and even managed the odd grin as Tiggy read out the words of sympathy that so often related how Diana had changed the lives of so many people. He even managed a smile and a joke at the number of playing cards, covered with the message 'Queen of Hearts' they had received. Harry told his brother they probably had enough for a full set by now.

At the end of that week, Prince Charles considered the boys to be coping well enough to be left on their own with Tiggy. Charles had decided to go back to public duties as his way of coping with Diana's death. Unlike his sons, Prince Charles had had experience of losing a loved one. He had been numb for weeks after the death of his beloved uncle, Lord Mountbatten, who was blown up by the IRA in 1979, but found work the best panacea for grief. On the same day that Lord Mountbatten was assassinated, 18 members of the Parachute Regiment were killed by the IRA in an ambush at

Warrenpoint, in Northern Ireland. To this day veteran Paras in Aldershot still talk with pride of the way Charles, despite the death of his most loved relative, took time out to visit, privately, the relatives of those massacred in the horrific incident. Prince Charles, who is Colonel-in-Chief of the Parachute Regiment, told them he grieved as much for the dead soldiers as his own uncle. The loyalty of the Parachute Regiment to their Colonel-in-Chief and future monarch has never faltered since.

Charles knew the boys now needed time on their own, but prior to starting work again he paid a heartfelt tribute to his sons and the way they had managed to endure the nightmare of their mother's death. 'I am unbelievably proud of the two of them,' he said. 'They are really quite remarkable. I think they have handled a very difficult time with enormous courage and the greatest possible dignity.'

Back at Highgrove, Harry and Tiggy would set off for long walks across the estate, usually ending at Highgrove Farm, where they would lean against the fence, reminiscing about the childhood games Harry and William played in the cow fields, or the disruption they would cause when the animals were taken to auction and Harry would be allowed to gently prod the rumps of the cows with a shepherd's crook. At one point Harry went in search of the magpie trap, but found it long gone. Like the plants he had once hoped would take root in his father's garden, willing them to grow to impress his dad, the magpie trap belonged to another time.

Sometimes Harry would sit alone in the walled garden, silently staring at the rows of sweet peas and beans his father lovingly cultivated and which he himself had helped to plant. The walled garden was Harry's place of remembrance. Years before, Prince Charles, proud of the way Harry enjoyed the garden almost as much as he did, had set aside that small area for Harry to dig around in. This small piece of land had quickly become neglected, but now Harry, searching for something to take his mind off the fact he would soon be going back to school, began digging up small weeds and clearing the overgrown flowers and dead beanshoots.

In November 1997, two months after Diana's death, Charles hastily rearranged his schedule to finally sort out a special treat he had been planning for Harry. Ever since they sat together in the walled garden when Harry was five years old, the prince and his son had spoken of visiting South Africa together. Harry, still obsessed by the events at Rorke's Drift and by now considered something of an expert on the whole Zulu campaign, was to accompany his father on a visit to meet the legendary African leader, Nelson Mandela.

Harry flew to South Africa with his schoolfriend Charlie Henderson and his best friend, Tiggy Legge-Bourke. The trio started the trip by going on safari in Botswana. It was the perfect antidote to the weeks of grieving that had followed his mother's death and Harry, thrilled by the wildlife of Africa, soon found himself enjoying Tiggy's company at least as much as his schoolfriend's. In many ways Harry and Tiggy took on the appearance of boy and girlfriend. They would hold hands during long walks in the bush, Harry protectively putting his arm around Tiggy as an inquisitive monkey came a little too near. As they clambered over fallen trees, Harry would chivalrously allow Tiggy to steady herself on his arm, and, back at camp, huddled around a log-fire, the pair would talk long into the dark African nights.

Harry and his father were reunited in Johannesburg, where the prince had arranged for the two of them to attend a concert by the Spice Girls. Like any heterosexual male, Harry was a fan of the five-piece girl band who had taken the world by storm with a mixture of bubblegum pop, sexy outfits and an uncanny, and irritating, ability to all talk at the same time that was strangely reminiscent of form 5c when the teacher leaves the room. They also came fully equipped with something called 'Girl Power', a rallying cry to the women of the world to take control of their own lives and not be manipulated by men. Record industry insiders allowed themselves a smile at 'Girl Power', knowing the Spice Girls were among the most manufactured bands in history.

Prior to the concert, Prince Charles told Harry he did not need to wear a suit, reflecting he might be more comfortable in his usual jeans and trainers. But Harry, showing an extraordinary grasp of media understanding, explained the press would then accuse Charles of trying to dress him as Diana would have done. Besides, he told his father, he felt more comfortable in his suit. Charles permitted himself a smile at this show of solidarity and told his son he was proud of him. Harry's reply had become something of a catchphrase between the two of them: 'Knock it off, Dad,' he laughed. Backstage after the show Harry allowed his father the honour of thanking the band for playing for free. He then watched with mirth as the five girls kissed and fondled Prince Charles to the great delight of the world's press.

Despite his initial shyness, Harry was secretly delighted when the girls began making a fuss over him too. Grinning broadly, he found it difficult to take his eyes off the much-flaunted cleavage of Geri Halliwell, AKA Ginger Spice, later describing her breasts to a school friend as 'massive'.

The rest of the trip was a staggering success, with Charles and Harry constantly demonstrating the type of knockabout humour and easiness with each other they had enjoyed since Harry was a small child. In a remote settlement called Dukuduku, Prince Charles sampled the local beer. Harry broke into peals of laughter as his father emerged from the mug with a frothy moustache, desperately trying to keep the strange brew down. The press commented on how relaxed Charles and Harry were, but to anyone who knew the royal family the pair were merely being their usual selves. Their double-act was a tribute to the family life both Charles and Diana had so desperately wanted for their children.

Harry and his father never got to visit Rorke's Drift. The relatively short time they spent on the African continent simply did not allow them the luxury of a private visit down to the Natal province. Instead, Harry was compensated with a large collection of Zulu souvenirs that included a large assortment of shields, spears and eating utensils. The gifts, some of which came from Nelson Mandela, are today kept in Harry's den at Highgrove. But one gift that Harry picked out himself was special. He had already learned from Zulu legend that he who gives a Zulu bracelet to the one he loves will always return to that love. Harry purchased a Zulu bracelet in Durban without telling his father. It was for Tiggy.

In March, 1998, the royal roadshow, hailed a stunning success in South Africa, travelled to Canada. This time Charles took both his sons, considering it a unique opportunity for them to witness first hand a royal visit. In a private meeting with the Queen prior to leaving for Canada, Charles asked if he was doing the right thing taking the boys on such a high-profile trip. He knew the pressure on the boys would be tremendous as they would be subjected to the full glare of the world's media. Her Majesty assured Charles the boys would cope, and reminded him how well they had managed when meeting the press and public in the immediate aftermath of their mother's death.

The welcome the boys received when they landed in Canada was staggering. The cheering, screaming crowd that greeted them was like a royal version of Beatlemania. One American female reporter watching the arrival was heard to mutter, 'If his name's Henry why do the Brits call him Harry?' to a collegue. A helpful member of the Royal Protection Squad leaned across and said, 'Henry's the other brother.' Looking puzzled the reporter asked, 'You mean there's William, Harry and Henry?'

'Yes,' replied the detective, somehow keeping a straight face.

'Jeez ... I never knew that,' said the reporter, shaking her head and scribbling into her notebook.

The boys' reactions to the crowds that seemed to grow in number at each venue were vastly different. Harry positively loved them, years of playing up to the camera in public and entertaining his family in private had prepared him for the adulation he craved. William, on the other hand, had watched his own mother succumb to this sort of attention and eventually grow to loathe it. William knew the dangers; the crowds lining the streets today would be buying the newspapers and magazines tomorrow that would be plastered with their pictures. Various periodicals would see their circulation rise once the boys were on the front cover and the vicious cycle that had so engulfed his mother would begin again. William, with a shrewd and wise head on his shoulders, knew very well the circus may have left town after his mother's death, but the paparazzi still owned the site.

Prince Charles was at first bemused by the reaction, but he knew, like William, it was a catch-22 situation. The more successful the boys were with the crowds the greater the demand to see them. The public would soon tire of official engagements and, like children in a candy store, would start asking for more. The press would step into the breach and a whole host of stories and pictures on the boys would quench the public's insatiable thirst for coverage. The paparazzi would then resort to the old 'supply and demand' chestnut that says, 'We're only giving the public what they want and besides, they didn't mind the coverage when it was for their benefit.'

Despite both Charles's and William's concerns, the trip was another spectacular success for Harry. In Vancouver the royal trio stayed together in a $1,500-a-night suite at the Waterfront Center Hotel. The hotel management, following advice from Prince Charles, had stocked the boys' room with a stereo and an extensive range of current pop CDs. Harry and William entertained themselves the first night peeking out of the window at the small crowd below and marking the girls out of ten.

The girls were everywhere. Teenagers, dressed provocatively despite the cold weather, who had got it into their heads all the boys had to do was see them and a hot royal romance would follow. Consequently a number of banners were held up wherever the boys went saying such things as 'William ... I'm the one for you'. In some cases, telephone numbers, hastily written on love-notes, were handed to the detectives and royal staff accompanying the boys. In all cases the letters were discreetly destroyed.

It was obvious, and not surprising, William was the heartthrob. With his stunning looks, inherited from his mother, he could easily be a movie star, but his beauty comes from a natural reluctance to accept he is attractive. A shy look, a glance up, and girls would melt in his presence. Harry, though not as conventionally good-looking as his brother, was also attractive to the hordes of young girls. In Harry they saw a rebel, the type of maverick machismo that women have found appealing ever since Clarke Gable told Vivian Leigh he didn't give a damn. In the words of one noted Fleet Street photographer, 'William is the perfect gentleman, but Harry is the type who'll go a little further after the girl has told him no.'

The difference in the boys' approach to the adulation that was at times clearly in danger of getting out of hand could clearly be seen during a trip to a high school in Burnaby. Thousands of fans had started gathering some six hours before the boys arrived. It wasn't exactly the warmest of weather and some of the young girls began to regret their decision to wear the shortest, tightest dress they could find. Harry acknowledged the crowds the moment he stepped from the car, grinning broadly and flapping his arms like a one-man Mexican wave. William, already growing more and more concerned by the vast numbers of young girls, refused to wave or even smile, trying to nip the adulation in the bud, like a modern day King Canute trying to hold back the waves. William was also increasingly aware of how quickly adulation could turn into its opposite. Young girls desperate to see their heroes do not take kindly to security staff trying to prevent them from doing so. Ugly incidents were reported of fans, deprived of a glimpse of William by the substantial numbers of police officers, turning nasty and hurling abuse within royal earshot.

William had also been appalled when the boys received a standing ovation simply for walking into a cafe. Prince Charles, bringing up the rear, could only groan. He had seen it all before with Diana and was beginning to share some of William's concerns. The rollercoaster that is fame had begun its climb to the top of the ride and was already preparing to come hurtling down the other side. Charles and his eldest sons exchanged glances each time the royal trip was mentioned on the TV or radio which, with the excessiveness of the North American media, was often. The situation wasn't helped by Harry, who thought it tremendous fun to deliberately guide

William towards the screaming teenyboppers. It led to one of their few serious rows with William threatening to get physical if Harry didn't stop it at once.

After a brief trip to the ski-slopes north of Vancouver, the royal party headed home. The trip had been a resounding success. Charles's popularity, which had hitherto been what one royal commentator described as 'up and down', was at an all-time high. It seemed as though he had been forgiven for his marital indiscretions by a public that could, at best, be described as 'fickle' when it came to matters royal.

But concern continued to grow in both Charles's and William's mind that Harry was seemingly oblivious to. They had now both been elevated to superstar status and, with each picture published in the world's press, the public's desire for more was increasing. The main problem Charles and his advisers faced when discussing the extensive media coverage of William and Harry was the same one they had faced at the start of Princess Diana's public life. The press weren't actually doing anything wrong. They were simply covering an official visit by three senior members of the royal family to a foreign country. St James's Palace could hardly blame Fleet Street for the fact that the trip was such a success and the public was suddenly demanding more pictures of the royals.

The press in Great Britain went out of its way not to overexpose William and Harry but, faced with pictures of William wearing a baseball cap back to front and saying, 'Yo dude!' to his father during an official photo call in Canada, they felt they had no choice but to publish – and publish BIG. The photos that came out of Canada during that particular visit were among the best ever recorded by Fleet Street's Canon Chorus. Shot after shot showed Harry, William and Charles performing their knockabout act in front of hundreds of spectators. As one veteran Fleet Street photographer put it: 'History will repeat itself. Prince Harry and Prince William will go on to be the biggest stars in the world and everything they do will come under the microscope. It's not our fault, it's not their fault ... it's not even the public's fault. But when a dormant volcano prepares to blow there is nothing you can do to stop it.'

CHAPTER TWELVE

During the Easter break of 1998, Harry's bodyguards became increasingly concerned about his behaviour. It wasn't something they could easily explain; Harry, though outwardly still showing the usual boisterousness one finds in every teenager, was becoming increasingly difficult in his attitude. He no longer cared to listen to the advice of his police minders, who considered such antics as driving a Range Rover up a slippery slope not the sort of activity a young man years away from a driving licence should be indulging in. And, for the first time, some members of staff at Highgrove had noticed something bordering on insolence creeping into Harry's behaviour. One royal estate worker who has known Harry since he was born said, 'Sometimes the wise-cracking comments that Harry was known for, didn't seem so funny ... It was almost as if he was taking the mickey, but in a hurtful way.'

Harry had also got into the unsociable habit of 'mooning' anyone he found himself at odds with. His behaviour, considered childish fun when he had orchestrated the mass mooning at Ludgrove so many years before, was not considered appropriate for a young man who was third in line to the throne. Charles, noticing that Harry's impish antics were no longer funny or cute, began to ask friends how to handle him, pointing out the concern among royal staff that one day the naked royal bottom on show may well be captured by a paparazzo's camera.

Charles arranged for the Spice Girls to pay a visit to Highgrove. Harry, who had last seen the girls in South Africa the previous November, would host a tea for the group. Charles crossed his fingers and hoped the young royal would not be lowering his trousers over cakes and coffee. The group flew to Gloucestershire by helicopter, landing on the lawn at Highgrove in a veritable gale that caused Victoria 'Posh' Spice to at first refuse to leave the chopper. The party was officially Prince Charles's way of thanking the girls for their continued support of the Prince's Trust charity, but Harry considered it 'his date' insisting on serving tea and offering wine from the Prince's well-stocked cellar. It did not go unnoticed among the girls how well informed Harry seemed to be on the wines of the world.

Charles became increasingly aware that he was filling the void left in Harry's life by Diana's death. Like a lot of parents who find themselves in an impossible position following a

Harry at the Royal Service.

Top left: The first of many pictures, Charles, Diana and the new-born Harry.

Top right: Harry with Princess Diana.

Bottom left: Every little prince's dream-come-true: Harry with the Spice Girls.

Bottom right: A rare quiet moment.

Term time.

Top: A family day at Eton.

Bottom left and right: Getting on with school life.

On holiday with Diana.

Top: On the slopes.

Bottom: In St Tropez.

A photo call for the royals during a skiing holiday.

Ahead of the game: Harry displaying his prowess on the polo field.

Top: Enjoying more sporting activities.

Bottom: A less traditional pastime: playing frisbee.

Top: In Klosters with his father and brother.

Bottom: Ready for the off: the mounted line-up before a match.

Keeping control.

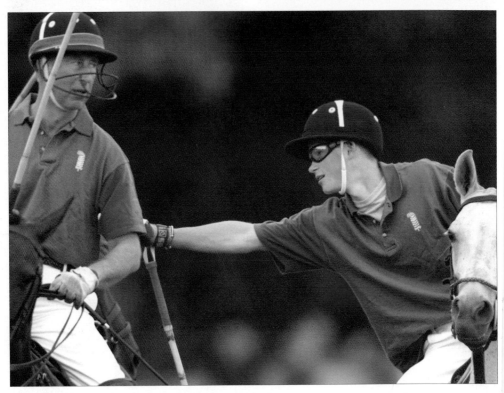

Top: Horsing around, father and son share a joke.

Bottom: But taking things seriously on the field.

Princes William and Harry.

Top: On the field once again.

Bottom: With his teammates.

In more relaxed moments.

Courage and dignity: the boys at their mother's funeral.

In official mode during the Queen's Jubilee celebrations, 2002.

The young prince.

partner's death, Charles now had to be father and mother to his two sons. In no way did he try to take over Diana's role, but, due to the enormous sympathy and respect he was given by the public, he found himself increasingly enjoying the type of fun days out he had usually left to Diana.

The boys were now living at St James' Palace, Prince Charles's London home that is situated on the Mall, within view of Buckingham Palace. The location allowed Charles to spend far more time with the boys. London being just 20 minutes from Eton, Charles had got into the habit, inspired by Diana, of shooting down the M4 at the weekend for a surprise visit.

On one occasion a group of German tourists enjoying afternoon tea at a cafe in Eton High Street were surprised when Prince Charles walked in with Harry. They sat at a table by the window and enjoyed scones and orange juice. After they had eaten, Charles ordered a pot of Earl Grey tea. Harry, not being such a tea snob as his father, ordered coffee. One onlooker said, 'They were just like any father and son enjoying each other's company. There were two detectives present, but they sat at a separate table and did not intrude.'

It did not go unnoticed, however, that the poor detectives handled the bill when the royal party left.

At the end of the Easter holidays, Charles took Harry and William to see Dame Edna Everage live in concert and found himself laughing hysterically when the outrageous Dame Edna began making cracks about the young royals dressing up in women's clothing. The idea of a cross-dressing prince caused much mirth in the audience and Charles found himself thoroughly enjoying his new role. Charles was also fit enough to take part in the football games that had resumed at Highgrove, though he refused to go in goal for fear of furthering damaging the arm he had broken at polo some ten years earlier.

But for all the fun they were now having as a family, concern continued to grow for Harry's increasingly disruptive behaviour. His grades at Ludgrove School had continued to slide and the decision had been taken to keep him back for a year. Harry was told, in no uncertain terms, if he wanted to join his elder brother at Eton, which he did, he would have to get there on merit and not assume his royal status would be an entrance ticket.

To the relief of both Prince Charles and William, Harry buckled down to his studies at Ludgrove and, in June of 1998, he successfully sat the Eton entrance exam. On 10 June, St James's Palace proclaimed, 'The Prince of Wales is delighted that Prince Harry has passed the Common Entrance Exam and has been accepted into Eton College.' The Palace added that Harry was 'thrilled' with his acceptance. They did not bother to add that Prince Charles was also thrilled and that, in a show of emotion, he had thrown his arms around Harry on hearing the news. 'Absolutely wonderful,' he gushed to his personal protection officer. Later that evening Harry, who was still talking excitedly of his Eton acceptance to his brother, received a call from the Queen, adding her own words of congratulations to the string of calls he had been taking all day.

But, as thrilled as Harry was, there was still some pain that went with the news. He knew, as William and Charles did, how much his mother had wanted both her sons to go to Eton. On Mother's Day Harry sent flowers to his mother's grave. Later that month of June, Harry, accompanied by Prince Charles and William, visited the island site at the Spencer family estate where Diana is buried. It was an emotional time for both the young princes, especially when they were shown around the as-yet-unopened museum in memory of Diana that Earl Spencer had completed as a personal tribute to his sister.

Knowing how emotional the visit had been, Prince Charles arranged for Harry to accompany him to France at the end of June to watch England play in the World Cup. The match, England's second game in the tournament, was against Colombia. Harry insisted on wearing an England scarf, a decision wholeheartedly endorsed by the Queen and Duke of Edinburgh, who urged Harry to support his team and ignore those royal courtiers who thought that such a display of patriotism for the England team may not sit too well in Scotland and Wales.

Harry watched from the stands as England won 2–0. Like most of the country he found himself screaming with delight when David Beckham scored his first ever England goal with a stunning free-kick. Live TV coverage showed Harry screaming with delight when the ball hit the back of the net, and jumping up with both arms above his head. Never before had a member of the royal family shown such emotion at a sporting event. For Harry, the Beckham goal was delicious, coming just a few weeks after Beckham's then girlfriend, now wife, Victoria 'Posh' Spice, had promised that her fiancé would score one for Harry. 'Once more into the net for Harry, England and St George,' he had laughed, though it is not known whether Victoria recognised the reference.

After the game, Harry got to meet a football legend: England's Bobby Charlton. Charlton, knighted by his country and considered by many to be soccer's only real gentleman, ribbed Harry when he learned that the young prince supported Arsenal. As a former Manchester United player it still peeved Bobby Charlton that Arsenal had recently done the League and Cup double, something Harry enjoyed reminding him about.

As the first summer without Diana came to an end Harry found himself closer than ever to his father. The pair, who had bonded so well together when Harry was very young, found they enjoyed each other's company. Charles, still suffering from a 'stuffy' image in the papers, went out of his way to keep Harry amused with a series of 'fun' outings that included a visit to the theatre to see the much-loved children's classic *Doctor Doolittle*.

But, for all of the football matches, theatre visits and fun days out, Harry had still to meet the woman his father loved, Camilla Parker Bowles. Despite the fact William had already met Camilla and, against all the odds, got on well with her, Charles was reluctant to introduce his mistress to his youngest son, fearing that the torture of seeing the woman who Diana had so loathed would be too much for Harry.

But, as it turned out, Charles's fears were completely unfounded. Harry met Camilla at Highgrove, the home where she had acted as lady of the house so many times when Diana was away. Despite an awkward start, with Camilla trying too hard to make conversation, Harry eventually warmed to her. He had been too young to understand the misery Camilla had caused his mother and, in any case, loved his father too much to hold any lasting resentment. Prince Charles was relieved when Harry and Camilla parted with a kiss. Now that both his sons had met the woman he was still so desperately in love with, and even the press seemed to be accepting Camilla as a permanent item, the prince felt a corner had been turned. His sons were both at Eton and Camilla was by his side, the future looked better than it had for many years.

Sitting alone in his study at Highgrove, the Prince of Wales reflected on how well things were going. In the post-Diana world, the public's perception of the royal family had changed. There were now two tiers of royalty; on one level Charles and his sons, along with the Queen and Queen Mother, were seen as the genuine article. Below them were the Edwards and Fergies and Princess Michaels, cannon fodder for the tabloids, grasping at an ever-dwindling civil list that was receiving constant cash-injections from the Queen herself.

Charles was relieved his own sons were free of scandal, indeed they were controlling things so well and with such dignity that, after the first anniversary of Diana's death, their contribution to the newspapers was made via a statement to the press through their spokesperson:

Throughout the last year, since the death of their mother, Prince William and Prince Harry have been enormously comforted by the public sympathy and support they have been given; it has meant a great deal to them, and they have asked me to express their thanks once again to everyone. They have also asked me to say they believe their mother would want people to now move on – because she would have known that constant reminders of her death can create nothing but pain to those she left behind. They therefore hope, very much, that their mother and her memory will finally be allowed to rest in peace.

One man who seemed determined not to move on was Mohammed Al Fayed. Having constructed yet another memorial to Dodi and Diana in the shop window at Harrods he had sent the latest in a long line of gifts to St James's Palace for the boys. They were returned unopened.

Despite the boys' ability to cope, major hiccups were just around the corner. At the beginning of August, Tiggy Legge-Bourke took Harry and William to visit her parents in Wales. During the two-day trip they visited the Grwyne Fawr reservoir. The steep 160-foot dam, which holds back more than 400 million gallons of water, is a popular spot for local abseilers. William had already been abseiling with the Combined Cadet Force at Eton and jokingly promised Harry he would one day show him how to perform what is, essentially, a dangerous sport. Daredevil Harry demanded to be allowed to have a go, despite the fact he had no proper mountaineering equipment and ignoring the lack of a special permit that climbers need to be allowed to abseil down the dam.

Ignorant of the dangers, and oblivious to the warnings of his bodyguard, Harry donned a harness and scaled down the steep drop headfirst, without a helmet, boots or a backup safety rope. It was, quite simply, a very dangerous and silly stunt, made worse by the fact that several tourists managed to snap off pictures of the very unprotected Prince Harry literally putting his life on the line to show off to Tiggy Legge-Bourke. Fleet Street, up until now reluctant to run stories and pictures on both William and Harry, found themselves with a set of pictures no right-minded newspaper could refuse. Despite protests from the Palace, and the criticisms of the broadsheets, the pictures were published, showing Harry perched precariously on the edge of the dam.

Prince Charles was furious, demanding to know why the bodyguards had allowed it and what on earth Tiggy was thinking of taking the boys to the dam in the first place. Feeling somewhat foolish, the royal protection officers pointed out to Prince Charles that they are only there to protect their charges and not to tell them what they can or can't do. Charles retorted that was hardly a logical argument when Harry was putting his life on the line in front of them.

Tiggy received a telling-off from the Prince of such severity that it made her cry. But Harry, the cause of all the trouble, ignored his father's words, insisting he was old enough to take care of himself and mocking his father's advice to 'take things easier'. Royal staff noticed that there was nothing compliant in Harry's manner. 'He simply looked as if he couldn't care less about all the trouble he had caused,' said one.

CHAPTER THIRTEEN

There are many buildings in Britain with breathtaking architecture. St Paul's Cathedral, the Natural History Museum, Buckingham Palace and a thousand others pay tribute to the magnificence of an empire that once covered a third of the globe. But there are none that convey the sentiment and history of that empire so instantly as the sprawling colleges of Eton. Standing proudly alongside the River Thames, perched in the shadow of Windsor Castle and surrounded by the playing fields on which the Battle of Waterloo is said to have been won, Eton College gives a lasting memory to the first-time viewer that is rivalled only by a sight such as the Manhattan skyline.

Everything about the college and hamlet of Eton smacks of history. Originally founded by Harry's namesake Henry VI, in

1440 with just 70 pupils, it became popular with the sons of the nobility in the seventeenth century. Since then, the cream of Britain's aristocracy has passed through the hallowed precincts of the ancient and illustrious college that, even today, cannot be looked upon without the strains of Blake's 'Jerusalem' coming to mind. From its earliest days, Eton College has enjoyed a close relationship with Britain's monarchy, supplying an almost endless line of advisers, servants, generals and admirals to the Crown. Queen Victoria so loved the place she would often take visiting heads of state on a tour of the grounds and the birthday of King George III is still celebrated on 4 June each year.

Prince William had started at Eton in September 1995 and was considered a model student, something his mother had taken great pride in as it was at her insistence he went there. It was not the royal connection that prompted Diana: the Spencer family has a tradition of attending the school, and both Diana's father and brother had boarded there.

On 2 September 1998 the world's press had gathered again at the college to welcome its newest pupil, Prince Harry. The photographers had started to gather early; word had already spread from the paparazzi to Fleet Street that Harry gave great picture. Harry was driven to Eton College by his father on his first day at his new school. He emerged from the car in the shadow of his new home wearing a light-green sports jacket and waving at the assembled press photographers, many of whom had been in the same position when his elder brother had arrived at the same spot three years before. There were also many members of the public who were delighted to receive grins and waves from Harry, turning on the charm for both cameras and fans alike as he had done since he was a child.

Harry was escorted into Manor House, his new home, by his father, to enjoy a light evening supper with his new housemaster Dr Andrew Gailey. Also in attendance were Dr Gailey's wife, Shauna, the house-matron Elizabeth Heathcote and an assortment of Harry's new schoolmates with their parents. From the start, Harry was determined to assert what he considered to be his new-found independence. At the ritual signing of the school's entrance book later that evening Prince Charles said to Harry, 'Make sure you sign in the right place,' to which Harry promptly replied, 'Shut up, Dad.'

After his father had left him on that first day, Harry made his way to the 10 x 7ft dorm room at Manor House. Looking out of the window, his view was slightly disrupted by the ivy that crawled up the wall, he noticed a few of the press photographers were still hanging around. He could not resist waving to them.

Unlike William, who was considered a model student by the time his younger brother started at Eton, Harry did not immediately endear himself to all of his fellow pupils. Indeed, several of them found him 'something of a prat' to begin with. One pupil who was in Harry's year said, 'The problem with Harry had nothing to do with him being royal; as long as I've known him he has never played up the fact he's a prince. He was just one of those kids who thinks he's really cool when he so obviously isn't.' He caused further problem with his irritating habit of constantly spitting in the street. 'He would do it through his teeth constantly. No matter where he was he would spit, even in the High Street in Windsor,' said a fellow pupil, 'it was the most disgusting habit.'

Harry asserted himself among the other boys not with his academic or diplomatic ability but by sheer brute force. In the playground he was the leader of the gang and quite prepared to use his fists to second the motion. He would swagger rather than walk. Always one step ahead of his friends, constantly and shiftily glancing around and sizing up the area, at times reminiscent of a south London drug dealer who finds himself on the wrong side of the river.

And he found himself the wrong side of the river many times. Over the bridge in Windsor he would calm down his tough guy act when confronted by the realities of a garrison town that still supplied the venue for Slough's Saturday night out. The combination of soldiers drinking heavily and young men whose attitude is, to put it charitably, somewhat aggressive after a few beers would often result in fighting on the waterfront on the Thames or, more often, at the taxi rank on the top of the hill.

Several times Harry witnessed scuffles and fighting in Windsor during nights out, invariably when he was on his way back to school. His friends noticed he was always reluctant to leave the action. Though he would never get involved (he wouldn't have been able to as his detective was always behind him), Harry would watch with a look of fascination as heavily made-up young ladies in micro-skirts and high heels implored their current boyfriends to 'Leave it, Duane ... he ain't wurth it'.

Harry saw himself as a fighter. In the playground he continued to ruthlessly push aside those he considered weaker than him. Indeed, Harry's desire to fight was at times almost suicidal, taking on boys far stronger and older than himself and emerging after a brief scuffle with either a triumphant smile or a defeated claim that the fight was a draw.

And it was the same on the sports field. Harry's style of playing football was naturally aggressive. But, as a defender, that aggression has to be kept in check. Harry would launch into tackles with an abandon that would leave his fellow players cringing and his opponents flattened.

Harry especially enjoyed the 'Wall game', the notorious sport, unique to Eton, that is a cross between football, rugby and all-out war. It is considered to be one of the most violent sports played among England's public schoolboys and was the sort of activity Harry positively relished. Press photographers who were invited to take pictures were stunned, as the young royal launched into the scrums and attacked the ball in an almost kamikaze fashion. One said, 'He had a look on his face that suggested he was quite prepared to kill to win ... It was actually quite frightening.'

The photographers comments were matched by a concerned spokesman for St James's Palace who said, after the game, 'Harry enjoyed himself very much,' and added, with an element of relief, 'He was doing a lot of kicking and it was a good match.' The relief was not without some foundation. Two pupils at Eton have died playing the game, which dates back to the 1780s. The sport has a set of highly complicated, and virtually unexplainable, rules that even those who have actually played it don't fully understand. It was no surprise when the match ended nil-nil, as there hasn't been a goal 'scored' since 1909 (and even that goal was highly controversial, with the defeated side claiming it had not crossed the line).

Harry was relatively unscathed when he left the pitch, and Eton's emergency services breathed a sigh of relief. The school's matron was getting quite used to patching up the young royal. Over the past two years he had been treated for a broken thumb, badly bruised arm, sprained ankle, two black eyes and a spinal injury that made it impossible for him to sit down for a week.

There was no doubting that he had inherited both his mother's and father's sporting prowess, but Harry's aggression was at times getting out of hand. When he attended a party at a friend's house, he managed to put his foot through a plate-glass door. St James's Palace was forced to release a statement about the incident after Harry was spotted walking around Eton on crutches. They claimed the injury came after Harry put his foot out to stop the door swinging back, but a fellow pupil at Eton insisted, 'Harry got involved in an argument with another guy over some girl and he kicked the door in sheer frustration.'

Whatever the truth of the matter, the injury was sufficiently serious for Harry to need hospital treatment. The cut, just above the shoe line on Harry's right foot, needed several stitches and kept Harry out of sporting activities for three weeks. It also alerted a number of freelance journalists, who make their living selling royal tittle-tattle, to the fact that

Harry was rapidly becoming a young man they should keep their eye on.

One journalist watched Harry chat up some girls in Eton High Street. 'He came out of chapel,' the reporter said, 'and he saw the girls sitting on the wall opposite. The only way to describe the way he crossed the road is "extremely cool". He knew exactly what he was doing and, within seconds of him talking to the girls, they were laughing ... For some reason he reminded me of a young Michael Caine, if Michael Caine had ever been cool.'

As the stories of Harry's aggression on and off the sports field began to filter through to Fleet Street, Britain's tabloid newspapers found themselves in something of a quandary. The editors, who had promised the public they would not pursue the young royal, were aware of a growing number of stories that were appearing in the foreign press. For some time before Princess Diana's death, canny pupils at Eton had supplemented their already extravagant allowances by selling stories to Fleet Street. When Harry joined his brother at Eton the practice continued, but the tabloids, all of which maintain a presence in the area, could not justify using them without being accused of unnecessarily invading the privacy of William and Harry. (Contrary to the public's belief, Fleet Street editors had actually treated Diana stories in the same way, refusing to publish pictures simply for the sake of it and only using stories that were relevant to the ongoing Windsor saga. Unfortunately, the practice created something of a catch-22 situation; the paparazzi, though grudgingly admiring the Fleet Street editors who were turning down pictures the rest of the world was publishing, were forced to maintain an ever-increasing vigil on Diana as the lucrative London market began to show signs of ending.)

It was, therefore, something of a dilemma for the *Mirror* when, just after Harry started at Eton, they were offered a set of pictures of the young prince in the High Street sporting a 'skinhead' haircut. To the vast majority of the public the pictures would simply have shown a young man following what was, at the time, the fashion of the day, inspired by football heroes such as David Beckham and Michael Owen. But, to Buckingham Palace, the pictures represented a serious breach of the somewhat ambiguous ground rules nobody had ever actually laid down.

The *Mirror*, not wishing to break its own embargo, carried out a classic Fleet Street compromise. They had already approached Buckingham Palace with their intention of publishing the photographs and learned that Prince Charles was beside himself with anger. Possibly hoping to avoid the Prince's wrath, and accusations of privacy invasion, their front page featured a computer-generated image of Harry with a shaved head, under the banner headline 'HARRY THE SKINHEAD'. It was innocent fun and should have been treated as just another piece of royal tittle-tattle, especially as it was quite good tittle-tattle and the sort of Fleet Street nonsense that inspires radio debates and phone-ins. Indeed, in another world, one could imagine Trevor McDonald saying at the end of the news, 'And finally ... Prince Harry has got a new haircut'

Instead uproar ensued. The *Mirror*, finding itself in the

unusual position of having public sympathy on its side, argued it had informed the Palace of its intention to run the story and picture, and that it could not possibly cause any harm or distress to either of the princes at Eton. It was simply the sort of story readers buy the tabloids for. The paper also pointed out that it had refrained from publishing royal stories many times over the past couple of years and had even turned down a particularly juicy tale concerning Harry's private life only days earlier.

But the Palace and Prince Charles were having none of it. An angry Prince of Wales retaliated by releasing a statement that said, 'The story and computer-generated pictures in the *Mirror* raise a general issue about the extent to which individual news stories about Prince William and Prince Harry cumulatively constitute an intrusion into their privacy. It is a matter of considerable concern to the Prince of Wales, who will be raising the matter with the chairman of the Press Complaints Commission and industry's Code of Practice Committee.'

The public's reaction to the statement was one of indifference. They found it difficult to criticise the *Mirror*, which was, after all, only reporting on a family that was fundamentally bankrolled by them. On the other hand, Prince Charles was only trying to prevent his sons from falling prey to the type of media overexposure that had so dogged Diana.

In footballing terms the incident had ended in a draw, though one could argue Prince Charles had scored the all-important away goal. The *Mirror* got away with its publication, but a warning shot had been fired across Fleet

Street's bows. The tabloid readers had shown they were prepared to tolerate royal stories as long as there appeared to be no permanent pursuits of the subjects. Prince Charles had made his point and received a sympathetic hearing from the public which, though concerned about Harry's and William's welfare, still wanted a good royal tale alongside their pictures of page 3 girls and stories of marital infidelity among Premier League footballers.

During a weekend break at Windsor Castle the Queen and the Duke of Edinburgh discussed the incident. They both knew Fleet Street's hands-off approach to the young royal would end the moment a solid story came in. Looking out of the window across the lawns, Her Majesty noticed the small gaggle of paparazzi that maintained an almost permanent vigil down by the Cambridge Gate when the monarch was at home.

'I really don't mind them being there,' the Queen had once remarked to her gatekeeper. 'At least I know where they are.'

Looking at the paps, she knew the same could not be said of Eton.

CHAPTER FOURTEEN

The somewhat shaky relationship between Prince Charles and Fleet Street was tested again the following week. The event was Charlie's 50th birthday. This event, usually relegated to the inside pages of the tabloids, had taken on extra significance in Fleet Street's eyes when word was leaked that Camilla Parker Bowles would be hosting the party. Even that fact may not have been considered important by the newspapers, after all, it was no longer a secret they were virtually living together at Highgrove when the boys were away, but it had already been revealed that both Prince Harry and Prince William would be at the party. This was to be the first time all three had met at anything approaching a 'public event'. (Fleet Street's interpretation of a public event is any occasion attended by *Daily Telegraph* photographers; if it's only the tabloids it's a star-studded event; if it's only the *Sun* it's an exclusive, and if it's only the *Express* it's been offered to everybody else but deemed not worth looking at.)

Following Camilla's advice, Highgrove had been transformed for the occasion. Professional caterers had decorated the outside of the house with wildflowers and foliage. In Charles's beloved walled garden, Greek statues had been erected, a personal touch from Camilla to Charles, who had recently read a book on Greek mythology recommended by his mistress.

Three hundred and forty of Charles's and Camilla's friends enjoyed the party. Many of these were seeing the pair at Highgrove together for the first time. Camilla was described by one guest as 'radiant, absolutely the most marvellous host'. A lot of people were surprised by how relaxed Camilla was at Highgrove, commenting on her almost telepathic ability to know exactly what part of the room Charles was in. Little did they realise that they had been carrying out the same roles in each other's company for many years.

The 'sounds' for the party were supplied by two wacky, baseball-cap-wearing dudes called William and Harry. William, taking charge as always, forced the chaste, elderly audience to dance to the remixes of DJ EZ and Norris Da Boss Windross. The two DJ desperadoes, at one point, were forced to suppress giggles when an elderly and titled lady misheard Harry's announcement of a 'groovy tune by Jason Kaye' as a 'moody tune by Jason and Kylie'. After leading her husband on to the floor she was somewhat surprised to hear up-to-the-minute rap blaring from the speakers and not her favourite Australian soap stars.

The highpoint of the party was the old show-stopper, 'YMCA'. The seventies hit by Village People never fails to fill the dance floor at weddings and birthday parties across Britain, and Charles's party was no exception. In vain did Harry and William try to show Charles how to do the faintly embarrassing hand movements that never quite seem to be done in unison. An English gathering dancing to 'YMCA' always resembles a convention of semaphore messengers sending pornographic e-mails.

Harry and William had one other turn that night. Secretly they had been rehearsing a spoof version of *The Full Monty*, the popular movie that featured a group of men stripping on stage. Harry and William were supposed to take off just a few items of clothing as the movie soundtrack played. Unfortunately for William, Harry, who had had a couple of drinks for Dutch courage, could not resist stripping off all his clothes and running among the guests naked.

Against all the odds the party was a resounding success. Both William and Harry were quite comfortable in Camilla's presence. Despite a thousand 'exclusives' that claimed to know the real story of Charles and Camilla's relationship, Harry and William had been aware of it for virtually all of their lives. Charles was now bearing the fruit of the honesty seed both he and Diana had planted long ago. 'I am very fond of Camilla,' he had once told Harry, 'but I will always love Mummy.'

Charles's love for Diana was genuine, right up to the very

end, and both his sons knew that. No matter what else had happened in their lives it was Diana who had given birth to the two children for whom Charles now lived. He could well remember the hours spent sitting watching William or Harry when they were very young, simply toying with a dinky car or frustratingly trying to force the wrong shape on to a jigsaw puzzle. Sometimes he would be joined by Diana and they would sit watching together, no words spoken, amazed by the sheer unadulterated joy a young child can bring to a couple simply by being there.

To William and Harry, Camilla had always been an 'adult' subject. They actually found it easier to accept Camilla than any of the fly-by-night suitors who seemed to be attracted to their mother, who only seemed to be interested in them as a means of getting to their mother. James Hewitt with his trips to army barracks and tall stories was always treated with suspicion by William and Harry, a suspicion that was eventually proved well-founded and turned to hate as Hewitt continues to sell the story of his romance with their mother for ever-diminishing amounts. Their cynicism also extended to England rugby captain Will Carling, whose presents of rugby shirts and scarves was a foretaste of Mohammed Fayed's attempts to curry favour with their mother by bearing gifts for her children.

Any dreams Fayed still retains about a relationship with William and Harry ended in disgust on the steps of the Palais de Justice in Paris on 5 June, 1998. Mistakenly believing he had taken over John Lennon's mantel as the nation's favourite working-class hero, Fayed arrived at the French courts to witness the testimony of nine photographers that were accused of chasing Princess Diana on that fateful night in Paris. Mohammed Fayed, his sombre black suit at odds with his beaming smile, acted as if he was the star witness rather than a mere onlooker whose official contribution to the investigation was to be kept as limited as the French authorities could manage. The Harrods boss had already given an undertaking to the senior magistrate Herve Stephan that he would trust the crash inquiry some months earlier. Since then, Fayed had consistently told journalists of his 'great confidence in the investigators'. It was fairly obvious to all that 'confidence' would evaporate very quickly if things didn't go his way. And things didn't go his way.

It all started to go wrong on the steps of the court when Fayed was totally ignored by Princess Diana's mother, Frances Shand-Kydd. Fayed had wrongly assumed the Spencer family would embrace him as the man who so very nearly became Diana's father-in-law. Unfortunately for him the family had no intention of being involved with a man whose continual stories of assassinations and dirty deeds were becoming an embarrassment and making a mockery of Diana's tragic death.

After the hearing, Fayed stormed out of the court and held an impromptu press conference on the steps outside. Seething with rage he said, 'She [Shand-Kydd] thinks she's the Queen of Sheba. I don't give a damn about her. People like her are on another planet.' As the journalists scribbled every word into their notebooks and the cameras flashed, Fayed warmed to his verbal assault: 'If she thinks she belongs to the royal family and doesn't want to talk to ordinary people like me that's up to her. I'm just a working-class guy ...'

Both Harry and William were deeply upset by the attack. Mrs Shand-Kydd was their other grandmother and, though the boys didn't see her that often, they knew Diana had loved her despite some typical mother/daughter problems that had at times tainted their relationship. Fayed's pavement tirade was the final nail in the coffin of his limited relationship with the boys, who both viewed it as 'despicable'. It was also the end of any involvement he had with the royal family as the Queen immediately ordered the removal of the 'by royal appointment' crown from Harrods

A week later Harry was back in the news, causing Prince Charles to once again look on aghast as the dam that held back the torrent of royal stories in the shape of Fleet Street's own embargo again began to leak.

This time Harry had been injured on the sports field during a particularly violent tackle at football. Harry, a defender, had always prided himself on the fact very few forwards found it easy to pass him. Indeed, Harry's style of play is reminiscent of the old style football hard-men like Tommy Smith or Dave Mackay. Allowing the striker to approach him, Harry holds back, not taking his eyes off the ball and watching the striker's body with his peripheral vision, waiting for the body language that will tell him which side the attacker is going round him and then lunging in with his left foot, taking either the ball, or the player's legs, away.

But all good defenders inevitably suffer injuries and Harry was no different. Finding himself flat on his back after jumping to head a ball and colliding with another player, Harry ignored the vicious stabs of pain that were shooting up his arm and played on. Later that night Harry, having been in agony all day, visited the school doctor who immediately diagnosed a badly bruised arm that could have been fractured. Harry had his arm dressed in a sling and was told to take things a little easier in future, advice that was immediately ignored when Harry threatened to 'fill in' a fellow pupil who laughed at his attempts to keep a blazer on with only one arm.

Determined to show off his latest war wound, Harry immediately set off down Eton High Street, regaling his mates, yet again, on the extent of his injuries and how he had heroically played on at football despite them. The walk was captured by a passing paparazzo who, surprisingly, had not been looking for royal targets. The snapper had fortuitously just been to the local photographic studio for film when he was suddenly presented with a laughing Prince Harry walking towards him with his arm in a sling.

The pictures were not printed but the story was. And once again it was the *Mirror* that enraged Charles. The Prince of Wales was furious and demanded an apology from the tabloid that was, once again, merely reporting an event after it had happened. The *Mirror*, getting slightly more aggressive, responded with an accusation that Prince Charles was trying to bully and censor the press. The powers that be at Buckingham Palace, including the Queen and Duke of Edinburgh, shook their heads in concern when they saw the *Mirror*'s response. For some reason the freedom of the press is a particularly sacred right in the United Kingdom and anything that threatens it is to be viewed with suspicion.

The *Mirror* had touched just the right chord with a public that was still, technically, grieving for Diana. If Charles could show any sign his boys were being harassed, the public would support him. But if the papers reported on an event witnessed by 21 other football players, assorted match officials and about 50 members of the public, how on earth could Buckingham Palace complain?

Charles was having none of it. His only concern was his boys, and he fired back: 'This matter is nothing at all to do with press freedom. Instead, it is everything to do with the privacy to which Harry and William are entitled during their education. It is about their ability to grow up without the telescope of publicity bearing down on their every move.' And, taking the fight right on to Fleet Street's front lawn, Charles wrote a letter to the *Mirror*, pointing out this was 'the third trivial and intrusive story about Prince Harry since he started at Eton'.

Charles continued:

Despite your argument that the public has the right to know about the health of Prince Harry, I can assure you there was absolutely no public interest whatever in the very minor bruising which Harry sustained. It was typical of the kind of injury which can happen to children up and down the country on the playing field. Indeed, each of the stories you have run about him concerned events which happen to many other children. Yet you sensationalise them to an extent which makes it very difficult for Prince Harry to have a normal life at his school.

Prince Charles's claims that he was only protecting his son's privacy were scoffed at among freelance journalists and photographers who had long ago given up on Fleet Street to publish anything to do with William and Harry. All of the tabloids had turned down pictures of Harry in a variety of sporting poses that had begun to circulate after he had started at Eton.

Despite Charles's concerns about the media's coverage of his children, he did have an awareness of and grudging respect for the way the newspapers had until now refused to publish stories that, five years ago, would have been major front-page exclusives. When the *Sun*, Britain's most notorious tabloid, was offered pictures of Harry being 'dunked' in a tank of water at a school fête they turned them down on the grounds they were taken 'on Eton time' and were therefore out of bounds.

Part of the dilemma facing both Fleet Street editors and Prince Charles was Harry himself, who continued to play up to the camera whether it was in front of a paparazzo or at an official photo call. While staying with the royal family at Sandringham at Christmas 2000, Harry led the royal party to church on Christmas morning. After the 40-minute service, Harry, accompanied by his father, insisted on meeting the crowds that had gathered outside the small white St Mary Magdalen's Church. Playing the crowds as skilfully as his mother had once done, Harry charmed all those he met with his genuine concern, asking how long they had waited and whether they were cold. With his usual knockabout humour, he told one woman he was heading back to Sandringham to watch the Queen's speech. Harry also charmed the watching press corps, which was delighted with a series of pictures that his father could hardly complain about this time.

Harry was also on form a week later, during the family's annual New Year break at Klosters, the super-rich ski resort in the Swiss Alps. Accompanied by his brother William and his beloved Tiggy, Harry arranged a photo-call for the press in exchange for being granted their privacy for the remainder of their stay. (These sorts of arrangements are quite common at the start of royal holidays and are always rigorously adhered to by Fleet Street. Unfortunately the paparazzi have no such agreement and wouldn't want one.) Clad in a stylish black ski suit and the obligatory baseball cap that was rapidly becoming his trademark, Harry showed off on the snowboard slopes with a series of intricate jumps and slides that left his father shaking his head in wonder. Both Harry and William had been determined to become expert on the snowboard ever since their father had told them he considered it glorified skateboarding. Harry and William, like so many other snowboarders who routinely had the same argument with skiers, knew the sport took just as much strength and skill as skiing.

Harry played up to the press on his snowboard, constantly looking around to make sure the snappers were taking pictures and knowing what they were getting would be splashed all over the papers tomorrow. But, to his father's continued annoyance, Harry never knew when to stop. Even if he spotted paparazzi lurking in the bushes at Eton he would perform, one time skidding sharply on his bike just yards from a paparazzo and then going back and doing it again, knowing the camera was trained on him. Harry's couldn't-care-less attitude where the paparazzi was concerned was probably the most effective way to defeat them. He was enabling paps to take pictures that would be offered to Fleet Street and turned down. Eventually the word spread along the grapevine of the paparazzi there was no point in taking pictures of Harry as there were too many on the market already.

When he returned to Eton for his second term, Harry had less influence over a new phenomenon which, he heard in hushed, secretive tones, was being played out in the changing rooms and dorms of the school. Two students would tie a cord around a willing third student's neck and pull it tighter and tighter until the victim passed out. The game, in some cases causing intense sexual gratification, was clearly extremely dangerous. At the point of passing out, the victim is, literally, having the life squeezed out of him, and has to rely on the common sense of two people who, by virtue of playing the game in the first place, have shown they have none.

Tragedy struck, as tragedy was always going to, on 22 February, when a 15-year-old student, Nicholas Taylor, tried to play the game on his own. The youngster killed himself with his bathrobe belt. Nicholas was sufficiently popular among pupils and happy at Eton to dismiss initial reports of a possible suicide. After the death of Nicholas Taylor, the school, wary of scandal and annoyed by the way the tabloid press had covered the story, ordered a crackdown. Prefects, including Prince William, were told any boy found participating in this stupidity would be expelled.

At around the same time, Harry had started gathering with other pupils on the sixth-form bench by the banks of the River Thames. Here, in the shadow of Windsor Castle, the pupils would pass around a hastily made joint, the unzipped cigarettes and torn off strips of cardboard on the floor beneath them. William would watch as Harry crossed the playing field with his mates, his hands in his pockets, a grin on his face, heading towards the Thames. William also knew Harry was beginning to spend time with Camilla Parker Bowles's son Tom Parker Bowles.

The 24-year-old Tom had recently been the subject of a major news story when he admitted using cocaine. It was later revealed that Tom Parker Bowles had been arrested for possession of marijuana and ecstasy while he was a student at Oxford in 1995. The story had given Prince Charles the chance to talk sternly about the dangers of drugs to both William and Harry. He had little idea that Harry's knowledge of Britain's drug problem far exceeded his own. To Prince Charles a joint was the first step on the slippery slope to drug addiction. To Harry, like so many other youngsters in so many other schools, a joint was something smoked to escape the daily drudgery of the classroom.

In May 2000, Harry watched his father play polo for a new team, Acclaim Entertainment. During the game, in which Charles managed to score a goal, Harry was spotted drinking with a teenage girl in the stands. At half-time, press photographers were astonished to see Harry, clad in khaki pants and a blue blazer, entertain his father with a series of mock karate moves. He then grabbed hold of his father's polo mallet and engaged in a lighthearted tug-of-war, clasping the mallet and refusing to let go.

Charles, aware of the photographers and the unique set of pictures that would be landing on every news editor's desk that afternoon, affectionately seized Harry for a long hug. It looked for all the world like a father and his son enjoying an afternoon's fun. In reality the hug gave Charles the chance to tell Harry to calm down, that he was in danger of making a fool of himself. But his words fell on deaf ears as Harry continued to lark about, entertaining the photographers in much the same way as his mother had done for years. He knew they could never get enough of this type of stuff, and appeared to be thoroughly enjoying himself. He also appeared possibly to be under the influence of drink.

After the pictures were splashed around the world in every major publication, Prince Charles knew that the genie was out of the bottle. Harry would be followed at every public, or semi-public, event by an ever-eager and more greedy paparazzi. It would be impossible to prevent more pictures appearing, as magazines and newspapers showed a considerable increase in sales as the public began to take notice of the hitherto unnoticed Harry.

Fleet Street had kept a discreet distance from both William and Harry since their mother's death. The boys were considered strictly off-limits to all paparazzi and press photographers, even when they were walking down a public street. It was almost as if Britain's press were going out of their way to show the public the boys would not suffer the type of over-exposure that had so upset their mother. The paparazzi, ever wary of a public that, though they no longer blamed them for Diana's death, still considered them sufficiently involved to be on permanent probation, ignored the potentially huge earnings currently running around the football pitch at Eton. As a result, during their tenure at Eton College, neither William nor Harry have been involved in a single ugly incident involving the press.

Unfortunately the same privacy was not granted to William when he began at his university, St Andrews, in Scotland. On his first week on campus he was harassed by a television crew that doggedly followed him throughout the day. William became so distressed by their presence he complained to his father, who rang up their boss and demanded to know, 'What the hell do you think you are doing?' It was relatively easy for Charles to do this, as the TV crew was employed by his brother, Prince Edward. St Andrews may well turn out to be a media nightmare for Prince William. In March of 2002 it was revealed TV celebrity Anne Robinson, strangely famous for insulting the guests on her top-rated show *The Weakest Link*, was due to become the new rector at the university.

But all the protection Charles had tried to provide for Harry and his brother, and the acceptance by Fleet Street that the boys were off-limits, disappeared on the day a senior member of staff at Highgrove sniffed the air and noticed the unmistakable aroma of cannabis. Prince Charles was immediately alerted to a fact that, though suspected by many, few were prepared to say. Harry was taking drugs. For the first time since the death of Diana, Charles had a major problem on his hands.

He wondered what Diana would have done. And then he spoke to William.

CHAPTER FIFTEEN

At 8.00am, on Sunday, 13 January 2002, a newsreader on the BBC World Service struck the first note of impending scandal. Following newspaper reports published in that day's papers, Buckingham Palace had confirmed Prince Henry of Wales had been sent to a rehab clinic by his concerned father after he admitted to smoking marijuana and to heavy under-age drinking. The sombre BBC voice, speaking in a tone that is usually reserved for royal deaths, said the matter had been dealt with by Prince Charles and Buckingham Palace considered the issue closed.

Exactly 30 seconds later, a DJ on one of London's local radio stations made the first reference to 'Harry Pot-head' and 'His Royal High-ness' and by lunchtime the majority of the population was aware of the story as the news swept across the country, helped along by the series of witticisms and ironic comments that are the staple diet of Sunday morning radio in Britain: 'Prince Harry and his father today issued a joint statement ... Royal security has been instructed to find the grass who leaked the story ... To buy dope in bulk do you go to the hash and Harry? ... The prince, known to his mates as Hash Harry ...' The merciless comments showed no signs of abating and certainly made a mockery of Buckingham Palace's claims that the issue was now closed.

Nobody is quite sure when Harry first smoked cannabis. Fellow pupils at Eton insist he smoked on the riverbank during the summer of 2000. Others claim it wasn't until May 2001 that Harry joined the furtive group of schoolboys sitting on the sixth-form bench with hands cupped to protect the joints from the winds that flew off the Thames. It was also reported that the young prince began smoking and drinking heavily when he was just 11 years old and sailing around the Greek coast on a luxury yacht. Though smoking is frowned upon by the royal family in general, there was no shortage of people in Harry's young life who smoked and made no attempt to conceal the fact. Tiggy had enjoyed a fag and would be sent outside at Highgrove to indulge the habit. Often Harry would stand with her while she smoked and, though there is no evidence to suggest she started him on the habit, watching somebody he loved dearly smoke must have had an influence on young Harry. James Hewitt was another smoker who felt no qualms about lighting up in front of the boys. Princess Diana would put aside her obvious dislike of smoking at KP when Hewitt was there; like so many people she indulged her lover's bad habit, choosing to ignore it rather than risk a confrontation. And, of course, Fergie enjoyed a fag, lighting up by the swimming pool at her home in Sunningdale when William and Harry were visiting, despite Diana's protestations not to do it in front of the children. Whether or not any of these people influenced Harry is not known, what is certain is that by the summer of 2001 Harry was indulging in cannabis on a regular basis and had also began enjoying an excessive amount of alcohol.

He had begun drinking at a pub called The Rattlebone, in the village of Sherston, near to Highgrove. In June of that year Harry fell in with a predictably loud, and at times aggressive, group of youngsters who enjoyed late-night lock-ins where the management did not appear to mind that the young royal getting exceedingly drunk in front of them was both under age and under the influence of drugs. For Harry, The Rattlebone was the perfect location to indulge his youthful fantasy – he was a tough guy. Swaggering around the pool table, he would invite spectators to take him on. Like a latter day Paul Newman in *The Hustler*, Harry would smoke cigarettes as he sent the balls cascading into the holes, cleaned up and asked, 'Who's next?'

One night, Harry became involved in a scuffle at The Rattlebone after repeated requests from the management to leave were ignored. Harry and his friends insisted on another drink before they left, but the bar staff, faced with an aggressive Prince Harry who had certainly had too much to drink, continued to press them to leave.

This followed another vicious encounter involving Harry

at the pool table earlier that week. A scuffle had broken out between Harry and two young men with whom he was playing pool, and it had been reported to the police. Following both incidents the management at The Rattlebone finally decided enough was enough, and Harry and his friends were barred from the pub for a short while, perhaps making young Harry the first royal to be locked out of an establishment since Charles I was famously denied entry to Parliament.

But being barred from what had very quickly become his local did not bother Harry. Back at Highgrove he still had his den, by now nicknamed 'Club H', where his friends could continue their drinking among the Zulu spears and Arsenal scarves that filled the walls. Harry had equipped Club H with a superior sound system and a well-stocked bar. He also filled the place with a number of young girls, any one of whom could easily find themselves suddenly locked in a passionate embrace by their host whose hands would wander seductively across their bodies with practised ease.

Indeed Harry was by now considered something of a prize by many of the local girls, who played the part of starstruck wannabes in order to get an invitation back to Highgrove at the end of the evening. Once there it was not unusual for Harry to have two or even three girls all over him. But Harry did not confine his amorous advances to gullible young teenagers. At a posh hunt ball held at Badminton House, Harry turned on the charm with 24-year-old Suzannah Harvey, a sometime model and TV presenter, who sold the story of Harry's seduction routine to the *Sunday People* newspaper.

Claiming Harry handled her 'like a grown man', Ms Harvey, whom the paper described as a 'stunning blonde', revealed how Harry had taken her outside for what can only be described as some serious necking, that included an awful lot of touching and fondling. For some reason the 'stunning' Ms Harvey and the wild Harry, whose kisses were, in Ms Harvey's words, so full of passion they made her mouth numb, did not take the encounter any further. Whether this was because Ms Harvey had suddenly had an attack of guilt about seducing a 17-year-old schoolboy or merely felt it prudent not to reveal the truth to *People* readers, her story had been doing the rounds of Fleet Street newsdesks for some time. There was an X-rated version of the story that Fleet Street journalists had been dining out on ever since it had first leaked. Unfortunately for *People* readers, the X-rated version was far better than the one they read.

Harry continued to enjoy a number of casual relationships with young girls who would be summoned back to Highgrove with the chat-up line 'Do you want to come back to my palace for a drink?' He knew no girl could resist the short drive back to Highgrove from The Rattlebone, where he was now allowed back in, and an evening's fun with the 17-year-old third in line to the throne. Like his royal predecessors from a bygone age, Harry would indulge in young ladies and then cast them off without a backwards glance. Many a young heart remains broken among the royal groupies who continue to hang around the pub in the hope of catching his eye. Their hopes were not all in vain. Harry has also been known to take girls out to the barns near the pub for a spot of touching and fondling that often ends with the young royal covered in straw, frantically brushing his hair. Back inside the pub Harry would continue drinking late into the night, often ending up dancing on the tables with his arms clasped around this or that beauty who would be waiting for the invitation back to Highgrove when Harry finally decided the evening, or, usually by now, early morning, should end.

Harry's behaviour continued to worry his protection officers but again they found themselves in that almost impossible position. They knew they were on hand only to protect their charge from danger; it was not their job to tell him what to do. The officers, many of whom had known a much quieter life when they had to protect the relatively easy Prince William, would watch in silent horror as Harry would knock back pints of Stella Artois lager with chasers of vodka and gin, knowing they were in for another drunken evening that usually ended with the youngster either being carried out to the car or drunkenly groping £50,000 worth of tabloid fodder. The police were also beginning to resent the fact they were being used as a taxi service for Harry's friends. At the end of each evening Harry would jump into the Royal Protection Squad's Range Rover with a clutch of friends and demand they be dropped off at their homes.

The final straw for the protection officers came one night at a friend's party that Harry, despite already being the worse for wear, insisted on attending. A full-scale alert was ordered when Harry went missing after a visit to the loo. Despite the fact that he was found almost immediately (outside on the lawn, drunkenly laughing to himself), the detectives felt that enough was enough and a delegation reported the incident to a senior officer. Unlike his new-found pals at The Rattlebone, time was now running out for Harry. From the days when Princess Diana had naively thought she was seeing James Hewitt in secret, nobody was listened to as much in royal circles as the Royal Protection Officers.

Prince Charles had spoken to William about Harry's drug-taking at Highgrove, and many of his immediate fears had been assuaged. He remained concerned, but considered it sufficiently unimportant not to warrant a full-scale head-to-head with his younger son immediately. Instead, acting on William's advice, Charles had decided to wait till the family holiday that summer when he would be able to speak to Harry 'man to man' about a problem with which, he admitted to his elder son, he was not entirely sure how to deal. Had it been merely a few puffs on the odd joint, he told William, he would have put it down to the natural excess of youth. A young man growing up has to be given his own space and allowed to make his own mistakes, he rationalised, remembering fondly how Diana would have simplified the problem.

William, showing an astonishing maturity, patiently explained to his father Harry's 'problems' were simply a phase any young person can go through. ('Jesus, Dad he supports Arsenal,' William joked, as if that explained everything.) The young William, tactfully pointing out that Charles himself had been thrashed at school for under-age drinking, reasoned with his father that it would be pointless to cause a major row over what was, to his mind, a relatively minor incident.

Prince Charles listened patiently to his elder son and asked him what the best way to handle it would be. Charles had already admitted to William he was shocked by how often Harry had apparently been using cannabis, and was man enough to admit he felt some way out of his depth. Sadly ignorant of the effects of the drug, Charles felt slightly better when William pointed out it was not a 'gateway' drug, one step away from heroin, but a minor league narcotic enjoyed by people of all ages. Indeed, many of Charles's friends probably indulged, William pointed out, and, considering the number of rock stars who had been invited to Highgrove, it's unlikely Harry was the first person to smoke pot at a royal residence. (The Beatles famously smoked pot in the toilet at Buckingham Palace, and Lord knows what was snorted during the drug-ravaged Victorian era.)

Charles continued to listen to his elder son with genuine interest. In a real way, William's wise words put the problem in perspective. Charles could clearly see how effectively Diana's policy of letting their children encounter the real world when they were young was now paying off. The job as adviser and consort to the king would fall on William's shoulders when Charles eventually took the throne and, if this was the shape of things to come, they would make a formidable team. Charles was also greatly relieved when William assured him he had never taken drugs.

Another nagging doubt for Charles, however, was the inevitable leaks to the press. Like William, Charles was aware Fleet Street newsdesks were receiving more and more tip-offs concerning Harry's troublesome behaviour and that it was only a matter of time before some ambitious news editor uttered the immortal newspaper phrase of 'publish and be damned.' But this current situation was different and Charles knew it. As head of several drug charities and a man who had visited hundreds of rehab centres in the course of his public work, he knew drugs continued to be a major concern for the British public. No Fleet Street editor could possibly turn down a story that involved the Prince of Wales's son, drugs and under-age drinking. Even a Hollywood scriptwriter would have too much material with that scenario.

Charles expressed his concerns about newspaper coverage to William. It was fortunate his elder son had grown in political awareness under the current Labour Government, led by the youthful Tony Blair, whose popularity was reflected in the Kennedyesque smile he held permanently in place. William, with all the expertise of the best government spin-doctors, shrewdly suggested that Harry attend a drug-rehab centre. It was not that Harry needed treatment, William stressed, but that spending time among people who had succumbed to the evils of major drugs would possibly give Harry a jolt. It would also bury the story the moment Fleet Street found out. Harry smokes drugs, Harry attends drug rehab clinic, Harry stops smoking drugs. Story over. It was simple and brilliant, and the type of PR campaign Max Clifford would smile at if he was capable of either a political campaign or smiling. It was a stunning success.

When Harry was told of the idea he readily agreed. Like any teenager who finds himself in serious trouble with a parent, he had feared the worst, something along the lines of the 20-year grounding his mother had threatened him with after his mass mooning at Ludgrove School. He also knew that William and Charles were right: when the press got hold of the story, as everybody knew they would, he wanted to be seen as a young man who had put his troubles behind him, not an out-of-control teenager with a penchant for fighting, drinking and drugs. That wasn't exactly the sort of image his mother had wanted and, if nothing else, Harry knew he was letting her down.

It was decided that Harry would go to Featherstone Lodge, a detox centre for heroin addicts, in south London. At the Lodge, Harry attended several group therapy sessions where he heard the horrors of drug addiction from people who were still, effectively, addicted and desperate for any treatment that would get them out of their own personal hell. Harry heard stories of addicts stealing their children's piggy banks in order to raise cash for their habits. And he heard of the nightmare that is 'cold turkey', the period of suffering every addict has to go through when they come off the drugs that is so bad many prefer the nightmare of addiction to the pain of release.

From the moment he arrived at the Lodge, Harry was stunned by how different it was from what he had expected. He first noticed the unusual silence that fills the air. There is no sound of life. No music or radios play; even the birds seem unnaturally silent. When Harry first arrived, accompanied by a detective, he was introduced to a former heroin addict who was to be his 'minder' for the visit. He was then shown all around the complex, visiting the residential rooms, where addicts and former addicts trade horror stories about their addiction, and the detox rooms, where addicts begin to regain the semblance of dignity that eventually gives them the courage to beat their addiction. Harry looked on in silence as he was informed that a lot of people never beat their addiction and spend the rest of their lives in rooms like these.

Harry remarked to his guide how surprised he was by the tidiness of the place and the absolute silence, which he found more unnerving than the drug horror stories. On a more mundane note, Harry noticed there was only one small television. As a young man who had enjoyed a 32-inch television screen all his life, Harry was quite shocked by this.

The visit also included the 'art room', where addicts go to express their feelings through drawings and paintings. The agonies expressed on the canvases, some of them vast murals with words such as 'CRACK' and 'HEROIN' written in blazing red, shocked Harry, who was reminded of some of the pictures smuggled out of German concentration camps that showed a similar suffering. Harry found he could take the stories of hell each addict supplied, but was left reeling by the simple word 'HELP' scrawled desperately across a canvas as an addict reached the very depths of despair.

Later, at a communal lunch, Harry talked face-to-face with a number of addicts. Though he appeared shy to the other members of the group, Harry eventually lightened up when he found how easy it was to join in the conversation. He discovered, like so many before him, talking is the easiest way to face up to a problem. One's own issues never seem so serious when face-to-face with the type of nightmare other people have to contend with on a daily basis.

Harry left the Lodge reeling from the experience. He knew his own use of drugs was somewhat amateurish compared to the addicts inside but he had learned one all-important lesson. An addict had told him, in no uncertain terms, there is no such thing as a casual drugs user. 'That,' Harry was told, 'is what everybody is at the start, a weekend junkie, but they are just a tadpole waiting to turn into a frog.'

Back at Highgrove, Harry met with Prince Charles and William. He told them he felt the visit had been a tremendous success and promised he would never touch drugs again. Then, ever the mischief-maker, he asked his father if they could release a 'joint' statement to the press. Both Charles and William laughed. It was good to see the visit had not ruined Harry's sense of humour.

The story of Harry's drink and drugs exploits, like so many stories, was broken by the *News of the World*, Britain's biggest-selling Sunday paper. Billed as a world exclusive, it was considered significant enough to be carried across seven pages and had employed the talents of the paper's two best reporters, Clive Goodman and Mazher Mahmood.

Goodman, the *News of the World*'s royal editor, is probably the only real royal reporter in Fleet Street today. Unlike his tabloid rivals, Goodman uses journalistic techniques that do not employ palace sources or close friends. Instead the dogged reporter, known as 'the dude' among Britain's paparazzi, patiently explores every whisper or rumour that his army of royal contacts provides with the same methodical approach that a homicide detective applies to the investigation of a murder. Glenn Harvey, a photographer who has worked with Goodman for many years, put it like this; 'If Goodman had been in business during the abdication crisis he would have splashed on it before the royal family had even heard of Wallis Simpson.' Thus it was Goodman who ruled the roost among the royal reporters, guaranteed first offerings from every photographer and freelance journalist on the street and produced so much royal copy each week that at times the *News of the World* resembled *Royalty* magazine.

Mazher Mahmood is another British newspaper legend. As head of the paper's investigative team, he reveals exclusives weekly on gangsters, drug dealers, spanking vicars and endless number of assorted perverts and criminals that are now more scared of Mahmood than they are of the Flying Squad. Some say he doesn't really exist, that Mazher is a front for a whole collection of investigative reporters at the *News of the World*, but he is sufficiently real to warrant a bodyguard, paid for by the paper.

The Harry story, like so many stories before it, had started with a tip from a contact, one of the army of contributors that the paper employs on a per-story basis. Months of investigation followed during which the paper built up a credible file on Harry's somewhat wayward lifestyle. He was drinking heavily, taking drugs and appeared to be suffering from some kind of personality disorder that was described by one journalist working on the tale as 'violent'. The paper had also discovered that Prince Charles, on hearing of his son's problems, had suggested that Harry attend a drug-rehab clinic where he could see first hand the nightmare world drug addicts descend into.

When the *News of the World* was printed that weekend, Buckingham Palace, already approached by the paper, was prepared for the story and the inevitable scandal that would follow. In some ways, on reading a first edition of the paper, royal courtiers were relieved. They immediately contacted Prince Charles to say the story was nowhere near as bad as they had thought it would be. Perhaps bowing to public pressure not to pursue the royals, following Diana's death, the *News of the World* handled their exclusive with sympathy and factual accuracy, standards for which Fleet Street is not normally noted.

Even more importantly, the crucial public reaction to lurid tales of royal drug-taking was firmly on the side of the newspaper. Throughout the country, concerned parents spoke to their children, finally realising that the entire issue of drug-taking was not confined to Glasgow housing estates and deprived parts of south London. If Prince Harry, with all his wealth and privilege, could gain a foothold on the slippery slope of drug abuse, surely their own children could.

The baby boomers of the sixties, who had previously ridiculed society's archaic approach to drugs, were now parents themselves and watched with mounting horror as young people appeared to indulge in drugs as casually as their parents had once abused snakebites and lager and lime. Periodically a drug death, be it heroin or the more trendy ecstasy, would be splashed across the front pages and sympathy would once again be given to a grief-stricken mum and dad whose son/daughter had 'everything to live for' and 'never touched drugs in his/her life'. In reality, of course, they obviously had touched drugs, which were now being consumed in huge quantities across the country by vast numbers of young people. It was estimated that up to 2 million clubbers were regularly taking ecstasy at the weekend and a recent surge in cocaine use had led to a dramatic decrease in the price. In London, coke could now be brought for as little as £50 a gram and in the suburbs, though heavily cut with any number of other substances, the drug was selling for as little as £30 a gram. Marijuana was so available that canny dealers were selling pre-rolled, slightly bedraggled joints for as little as £1.

Every young person heading for the pubs and clubs of their hometown each weekend was aware of drugs, what they were, how much they cost, where to get them. Even those who did not indulge knew exactly what was going on when furtive exchanges of cash and little white packets took place at the back of clubs or even, in some cases, openly across the bar of a pub. It was, therefore, almost a relief for some parents to see the huge banner headline 'HARRY'S DRUG SHAME' splashed across the *News of the World* that Sunday. Now the entire issue of drug-taking could be put into context and discussed openly as more and more parents finally, and reluctantly, began to accept that they could be the next sad couple who sat at the hastily arranged press conference and tearfully said, 'We had no idea our son/daughter was doing heroin/cocaine/ecstasy.'

The story was welcomed for another reason. The British public, long immune to scandals involving the royal family, were glad of a chance to read page after page of Harry's drug revelations. It finally took their minds off the news story that had dominated the world for the past three months, and a Christmas many had felt no great desire to celebrate. The image that had persisted in the public consciousness until now was one of total destruction, of a city in mourning, of people in pain ... of a mighty country humbled and a date that was now permanently stamped in every living person's mind, as the world still tried to come to terms with the terrible events of 11 September.

For a few hours, Harry's concerned face on the front page of the *News of the World* took the public's mind off something far graver, and it was immeasurably grateful for that. In Britain, a country that had somehow managed to survive the Blitz, the front page of the *News of the World* that sunny Sunday morning meant the past three months of troop deployment, diplomatic missions and armed conflict were now behind them, and an almost audible collective sigh of relief swept across the country.

CHAPTER SIXTEEN

On a cold Saturday night in March, Prince Harry found himself on the riverbank of the Thames with a fellow pupil. The boys were dressed in NATO camouflage, their faces blackened. Both were taking part in a military exercise organised by the Combined Cadet Force, the military arm of all Britain's public schools. Harry, coming from a family steeped in military history, loved the CCF. He saw it as a prerequisite for the day, some time after he completed university studies, when he could join the army for real, something he had discussed many times with his father. Harry desperately wants to join the Paras, but his dad, following discussions with royal advisers, is not too keen on the idea. It has been pointed out to Harry several times that the Paras, as the spearhead of the British army, get to see action considerably more than most regiments, and the idea of the third in line to the throne on combat duties in the Balkans or Africa continues to fill senior royal advisers with dread, especially when Harry's response to the concern has been: 'But that's exactly what I want to join the Paras for ...'

His father, not wishing to thwart Harry's dream by persuading him against a military career, prefers to leave the problem at least until Harry completes his studies at Eton. Charles is known to favour the idea of Harry joining a smaller regiment, possibly the Welsh Guards, but is equally aware of his younger son's stubbornness in the matter. A friend in Harry's class at Eton said, 'For Harry, the army means action, action, action. He doesn't want to be seen as just another royal doing a stint in the services in order to gain a few medals and be allowed to wear a uniform on royal duties. He genuinely looks on it as a career. Like his uncle Andrew, he wants to do the full 22 years, and if that involves going to war then so be it. Let's face it, over the past year, Harry's probably been involved in more scrapes than the Paras anyway.'

Harry could not wait to get into the CCF, which is open to all members of the lower sixth. Within six weeks of joining, Harry had been promoted to Lance Corporal and is heavily tipped to be an officer by the end of his Eton studies. The cream of the CCF, the junior officers, are often lured to Sandhurst when they leave school and Harry has already discussed with his father a commission into the army as part of his university studies.

As Harry waited by the Thames that night in March he couldn't help showing his nerves. His companion was beginning to irritate him by constantly asking the time. Both boys knew the designated start of the exercise was approaching and that they were probably in for a hard time. 'Shut up,' said Harry, as his comrade asked again what time it was. 'Be patient.'

Suddenly Harry looked up and was confronted by five 'members of the Taliban' armed with AK47s and screaming, strangely in perfect English, 'Get your fucking hands up the pair of you.' Harry did as he was told, raising his arms above his head and, following instructions that included an awful lot of Anglo-Saxon profanity, dropping to his knees. Harry was dragged up the riverbank and a hood was placed over his head. Gruff and hostile hands then propelled him towards a Land Rover, and all the time the obscenities were being shouted in his ear.

Both boys were taken to a small shed situated in the tiny hamlet of Bovney, next to the River Thames. There they were held as hostages while a unit from the CCF, under the guidance of a professional soldier, set out to rescue them. The unit had been given map references and co-ordinates of where the hostages were being held. In the meantime, Harry and his companion were forced to undergo intense interrogation at the hands of the 'Taliban'. The exercise, known as 'escape and evasion' is twofold. Firstly, the rescuers have to carry out a reconnaissance mission to establish where the hostages are being held, then they have to rescue them before the enemy manages to get vital information from its prisoners.

Harry was kept hooded throughout the nine-hour ordeal.

He was also forced to stand in what Northern Ireland veterans refer to as the 'stress position', an extremely uncomfortable stance whereby a prisoner is forced to lean against a wall by his fingertips with his legs outstretched behind him. A soldier who took part in the exercise said, 'The stress position is an absolute nightmare. After just a few moments the backbone feels like it is starting to break, your fingers start to burn with the agony of trying to support your whole body and, with your legs outstretched, the victim is prone to a good kick between the legs. And all the time the enemy is screaming in your ears, demanding information ... Even men trying to join the SAS have found this part of the training the hardest.'

The psychological torture Harry was forced to endure was intense, but he never gave away any information. Following his training, and impressing his captors, Harry politely refused to divulge anything, claiming, correctly, that as a prisoner of war he only had to reveal his name, rank and place of birth. The soldier who took part in the exercise said, 'Even though he was showing signs of strain and disorientation, Harry repeatedly replied, "I'm sorry, sir, I cannot answer that question," which is exactly what a soldier is trained to do.'

As the night dragged on, and there was no sign of the rescuers, it was clear that Harry still had no intention of giving in. Despite feeling tired, humiliated and alone – he had been split up from his companion straight away – he again refused to talk. At times close to tears, he continued to say, 'I'm sorry, sir, I cannot answer that question,' in response to the interrogation, which was becoming increasingly hostile as the

Taliban began to realise that time was running out. Guards outside the shed had already reported movement on the other side of the Thames and felt they would be coming under attack very soon.

Harry was dragged out of the shed and moved to a new location closer to the college just moments before his comrades crossed the river. By now the interrogators had given up on getting any information out of him and were merely trying to stop him from being rescued. In this they were successful. Despite finding the original shed where Harry was held, the rescue mission ultimately failed, as the terrorists managed to avoid detection and finally dumped Harry on the grounds of Eton College at 5am.

Despite the failure of the rescue bid Harry was given glowing reports from his superior officers, who commented on his natural ability at soldiering. He was by now considered to be one of the best cadets and firmly on course to gain the prestigious Sword of Honour, an award given each year to the best cadet at an elaborate passing-out ceremony on college grounds.

The sword is something Harry has set his heart on winning ever since his brother, William, received the honour in the summer of 2000. But, even more importantly for Harry, his aptitude and excellent reports throughout his CCF activities have brought his name to the attention of the senior ranks of the British army. One soldier, who has trained alongside Harry, said, 'There is no question Harry won't go in the army. He loves the life and now knows he can have the pick of Britain's best regiments. In many ways good officers are like football players. Their potential is spotted early on and they are then sought after by the best regiments. Harry can now have the pick of the finest.'

A career in the army had already been discussed between Harry and his father and, though Charles was keen for his son to spend some time in the military, he has also mentioned some sort of academic role that would exploit Harry's extensive grasp of military history. 'Maybe I could teach history at Oxford,' Harry once laughed. The idea brought a smile to Charles's face, as he added, 'Or Harvard?' It was said in jest but a seed had been planted in both of their minds.

Exactly what Harry was going to do when he finished his education was a topic that had been discussed many times with his father. Charles could already see a problem with the military. Harry was showing interest only in those regiments that are immediately propelled into the front line when the fighting starts. Though the royal family has a rich tradition of supplying fighting men (Prince Andrew was famously hailed a hero during the Falklands war when, as a pilot, he used his helicopter as a decoy against incoming missiles whilst troops were evacuated from a burning ship), but concerned advisers pointed out that under the current Labour Government, British soldiers were being deployed in the world's trouble spots at an alarming rate. If Harry was to serve in a regiment such as the Paras as an officer, the chances are he would have to do his fair share of active service. There was no suggestion from either Charles or the advisers that Harry be kept away from the fighting if that is what was called for. The concern was that Harry would actively want to go to battle. Prince

Charles could easily see his son in the same position as the legendary Colonel H, a parachute officer killed during the Falklands as he single-handedly charged an Argentinean machine gun post.

Apart from the armed forces, another option for Harry is to take on a role within the Prince's Trust, the Prince of Wales's own fund that gives young people the chance to realise their dreams through their own work. The Trust, set up in 1976, has been a staggering success and remains Prince Charles's proudest achievement. Its aims are not only to help young people set up their own businesses, but to give them a chance to express their own abilities and potential as they do so. The vast majority of young people who receive financial help from the Trust are from disadvantaged sectors of the community, predominantly the unemployed and the disabled. Priority is also given to those troubled youths who come from broken homes or have spent time in care. Annually, grants totalling £10 million are handed out to youngsters, all aged between 14 and 25, who are then encouraged to make their own decisions and develop their own skills.

Prince Charles knows that Harry's natural gift for communication with people of his own age would be an asset to the Trust. Many times Prince Charles has looked on with pride as Harry cuts through the stuffy protocol of royal life by slapping palms with his peers rather than shaking hands. He is also a natural organiser, especially at team events. Whenever a game of football was hastily arranged at either Highgrove or KP, it was always Harry who put the shirts down for goalposts and then announced where the area of play was. Delegating players to each side, Harry would prepare to kick off with a shout of: 'Five goals each way, change ends at half-time and we'll be Arsenal.'

The ease with which Harry makes friends would come in handy for organising the huge sports tournaments and rock events the Trust is dependent on for donations. It would also be tremendous fun. Even Harry, whose attention span is said by close friends to be 'somewhat limited', would not get bored flying around the country trying to get Atomic Kitten or Kylie to perform for him.

With his drinking and drug-taking exploits behind him, and a series of extensive and important exams on the horizon, Harry returned to Eton after Christmas 2001 determined to make a new start. Fellow pupils noticed a subtle change in the youngster they had once considered a 'bit of a prat'. Gone was the swagger, the aggression, the attempts to play the tough guy. In place of these, there was a Harry who was more gentle, quieter. He was prepared to listen to others and no longer wanted to be the centre of attention. It was almost as though he knew he had been lucky with the press coverage. The one thing both Harry and William had dreaded was that the world's press would blame Charles, castigating him as an unloving father and claiming none of it would have happened if Diana was alive. To their relief, and to Fleet Street's credit, this did not happen. The coverage was very sympathetic to Charles and paid tribute to William's part. In a leader comment in the *News of the World* the paper referred to Charles as a 'wise and loving dad' and commended the 'refreshing courage and honesty of the Prince of Wales'.

Harry, who loves his dad more than anyone else on earth, read that and knew he had let his father down and resolved not to do it again.

He had also taken up golf. Encouraged by his uncle Andrew, who spends more time on a golf course than Tiger Woods, Harry began playing at Eton golf course with three pals after school. With his obvious sporting ability, Harry found himself a natural golfer despite his initial frustrations at teeing off. Harry discovered a quite brilliant aptitude for 'slicing' the ball almost to a 45-degree angle.

'If I aim at Windsor Castle,' he told his golfing partner, pointing to the castle a mile away to his left, 'I'll have a fair chance of getting it on the green.' He grinned, nodding towards the flag about 50 yards in front of him.

Harry's excessive 'slice' was eventually sorted out by his uncle Andrew, who, after years of experience, pointed out that success in any sport played with a round ball comes down to technique, not brute force. If you hit a golf ball or a football or even a cricket ball with everything you've got it won't go anywhere.

Playing a round on the golf course was infinitely more enjoyable than getting in the rounds at The Rattlebone, Harry discovered, and it didn't leave any sort of hangover. After being told he could now use the nine-hole golf course at Windsor Castle, he became determined to prove to his father that his days of excess were behind him. Harry's chance to show his father his new-found maturity came sooner than expected. On Saturday, 31 March, as Charles and his sons enjoyed their annual Easter holiday on the ski-slopes of

Kloster's, Switzerland, the news came through from London that the Queen Mother had died.

Both Harry and William were with their father when he was told the news he had dreaded for so long. They watched as he broke down in tears, bemoaning the loss of his beloved grandmother, his face a picture of agony. Charles held his sons tightly as he wept, reaching out to them. William and Harry exchanged knowing glances, their father needed them now. He needed their support and help to get through his loss. He could not have wished for two better supporters: both of them knew only too well what he was going through.

The death of the nation's favourite grandmother produced a wave of patriotism that swept across the country. People immediately began to mass outside Buckingham Palace in an atmosphere of stunned silence, coupled with pride and the fondest of memories. Many of the mourners were old hands and had stood on the same spot at successive royal events. They remembered the Coronation, the young Queen and her handsome husband waving from the balcony above them. They remembered Churchill's funeral, sobbing for the nation's greatest wartime leader; they remembered the Silver Jubilee when, despite the best efforts of the Sex Pistols, they celebrated 25 years of Queen Elizabeth's reign without appearing preposterous, and they remembered a day drenched in sunshine back in 1981 when they watched and cheered as Prince Charles kissed his new bride in front of them. Now they stood together, remembering the woman who had been there through all those events and more. Veterans of the war, medal ribbons proudly displayed, spoke for their fallen comrades as they told foreign TV crews, 'She never let us down, she was a right good 'un ... Gawd bless 'er.' And the old women, many of whom had spent night after night hiding from German shells during the worst days of the Blitz remembered the inspirational and immortal words the Queen Mother had spoken when the suggestion of getting the royal family out of Britain was first suggested. 'I will not leave the King,' she replied, 'and the King will never leave the country.'

When they buried the Queen Mother just over a week later, Great Britain put on a show the like of which no other country on earth is capable of producing. It wasn't just a funeral, it was a celebration and a chance for an entire country to say goodbye and thank you to a woman who had come to be symbolic of the greatest generation the United Kingdom has ever produced.

Prince Harry watched the preparations for the Queen Mother's funeral with something approaching amazement. It was the first time he had witnessed the enormous respect the world pays Great Britain when the country uses a state occasion to flex its muscles. As Harry walked behind the Queen Mother's coffin on its last, sad journey down the Mall, he could not help glancing up at the thousands of silent mourners who were as vital and as relevant to this spectacle as the massed brigades of the Guards. The last time he had made this walk he had been behind his mother's coffin. Now, the memory of that terrible day was being replaced by an overwhelming sense of pride. He glanced across to his brother, William, standing beside him. Sombrely dressed in a grey morning suit, William was looking for all the world like the King in Waiting that he is. Although William had so far provided most of the support to Harry, they both knew that would change. As the younger brother to the king, Harry's royal role in life will be that of the eternal substitute, constantly on the bench and hoping to God he never gets called on to the pitch. But the adversity the two boys faced together in the shape of their mother's death has formed a bond of mutual trust and understanding that is both precious and formidable. In some ways they are reminiscent of those veteran Lancaster bomber crews whose average age, after 25 missions, was still only 21. Diana's death robbed the boys of parts of their childhood as surely as the war destroyed the innocence of those other young men's youth.

Somewhere in the world today there are two young ladies, probably still in their teens, who will also take on the role that William and Harry have designated each other, that of the best friend. Whoever they are, these two future princesses that will join this unique, two-piece, happy band of brothers, they will discover that both Harry and William have already been loved beyond reason by a woman they will forever be compared to, their mother Diana. It was Diana's love that has made Harry and William what they are today: two sons in whom she would have taken enormous pride. Her gift to them was unique, a mother's love; her gift to the country was equally unique, two princes that will take the British monarchy well into the middle of the century and a legacy that will go far beyond.

Now, as the country said goodbye to a woman and an age that will never come again, the Queen, in the autumn of her reign, began to look forward to the Golden Jubilee celebrations she had been so busy preparing for, and in which her mother had been so keen to take part. As the cortege went into Westminster Hall, the Queen Mother's coffin finally slipped from view. Behind her, Charles, Harry and William followed, and fleetingly the trio was framed in the magnificent archway. It was a symbolic moment. The old order had given way to the new.

CHAPTER SEVENTEEN

When the writer Hunter Davies completed the official biography of the Beatles in 1968, he carefully decided against predicting what the future held for the band that was already the most successful in rock history. His decision was vindicated by the group's squalid collapse just a year later, an occurrence nobody had anticipated when the biography was first published, and an event that would have made the book all but redundant if it had included predictions on a future for the Fab Four.

I tend to agree with Hunter Davies. Trying to predict the future for Prince Harry too precisely at this point in his life is not a useful exercise and it could well turn out to be an inaccurate one. We know certain things, for instance, that he is determined to finish his studies at Eton and then follow his brother to St Andrew's University, in Scotland. Harry has already discussed with his father his intention of taking a gap year abroad between ending college and starting university as his elder brother did.

As discussed, Harry wants a career in the army, and in this he has been backed all the way by both his father and the Duke of Edinburgh. The Duke, in particular, has spoken to Harry at length about the many possible regiments that would enjoy the prestige and publicity of having a prince in their ranks. Harry's desire for a career in the Paras has already been questioned by his father, who was told to discourage his son from that regiment by the Duke of Edinburgh. Charles and his father had been walking in the grounds at Balmoral when the subject of the Paras came up. Charles asked his father what he was supposed to do if Harry insisted on the Parachute Regiment. 'Well, you're Colonel-in-Chief of the Paras ... just say you don't want to be accused of nepotism,' quipped the Duke.

As most of the world now knows, Harry has already shown more than a passing interest in wine, women and song – the royal Mick Jagger to big brother William's Cliff Richard. And yet, as we saw at both the Queen Mum's funeral and the Golden Jubilee celebrations, Harry has inherited his father's deep sense of duty, a kinship shared with William who, when standing alongside Harry, offers the world a brief glimpse into the future and the formidable strength the pair will have as senior members of the royal family.

As we grow to admire the two young princes more and more, seeing them almost daily in an ever-growing number of what appear to be officially sanctioned press photographs, we should perhaps reflect on the success of their mother's promise that they would grow up 'like normal children'. With all due respect to Prince Charles who has been, and continues to be, a magnificent father to both his children, it is Diana's influence that has shaped the boys' lives most of all. Without her, Harry and William would have suffered the type of traditional royal upbringing that was so loathed by Prince Charles.

Knowing what we do today, it is hard to watch the television footage of a five-year-old Prince Charles meeting his mother as she arrives back from a long overseas tour. Stiffly, almost painfully, the monarch offers her hand to be shaken by a little boy who wants only to jump into his mother's arms and be treated like the child he so obviously is. Compare this with the uninhibited, spontaneous joy on Princess Diana's face as she launched herself at her children in front of the cameras on the Royal Yacht Brittania in Canada. Diana hated every moment she was away from her boys and yet, somehow, she managed to smother them with love without spoiling them.

This is not to say that the Queen has been anything but a good mother. As I discovered again and again whilst researching this book, the Queen and all her children enjoy a loving relationship that is no different to that of any other family. The difference is that they are the royal family and are therefore, publicly at least, trapped in a world where tradition and protocol are the orders of the day.

Many people disagreed with the Queen's original refusal to allow the flag at Buckingham Palace to fly at half-mast following Diana's death, assuming it was some kind of personal slight on Diana. In fact it was the correct thing to do. There are certain rules and regulations that govern the running of a monarchy within a democracy like Great Britain and the golden law, very similar to the judicial system, is that personal feelings cannot force a precedent to be changed. The woman called Elizabeth, left alone at Balmoral with two grief-stricken children, would have done anything to alleviate their suffering; but that same woman in the role of monarch could not allow such an unprecedented break with tradition as the lowering of the flag, no matter how much criticism she faced.

In brutal terms, and using the argument the Queen herself used against her advisers, if the flag at Buckingham Palace could not be lowered for Winston Churchill's funeral how can it be lowered for a woman who, at the time of her death, wasn't even a member of the royal family? Even the most die-hard Diana fanatic would agree that, in the great scheme of things, a man who inspired Great Britain's finest hour and led the country through its darkest days, is more worthy of that tribute. The final verdict on allowing the flag to be lowered was initiated by Prince Charles. Her Majesty simply agreed with him when he pointed out that the general consensus among her advisers was that Diana's death was unprecedented and therefore no precedents would be set or broken. It is fairly obvious that Fergie or Edward's death would not prompt the type of universal mourning that followed Diana's, and nobody would be calling for any flags to be lowered at Buckingham Palace for them.

The Queen also found herself facing criticism for not rushing down to London in the immediate aftermath of Diana's death, preferring to stay at Balmoral with William and Harry, and to maintain a dignified royal silence. Many people considered this to be a gross error and an insult to Diana's memory. This criticism reached its climax with a front-page headline in the *Daily Mirror* that screamed 'SPEAK TO US MA'AM ... YOUR PEOPLE ARE SUFFERING', a headline that perfectly captured the mood of the British public who, for the first time ever, were turning on the monarch they loved with unprecedented anger (Newspaper polls were already showing two out of three people believed Diana's death would bring down the monarchy.)

But the Queen rode the storm. She knew two things the angry leader writers in the tabloids did not. Firstly, the anger and grief over Diana's death would abate and therefore impulsive decisions taken now would be regretted later. Secondly, and far more importantly, William and Harry wanted to be with her in the safety and seclusion of Balmoral. There were still too many tears to be cried for them to be left alone, and Prince Charles, though grief-stricken himself, had to be available to the many courtiers and government officials that were now planning a funeral that would be a state occasion in all but name. Unfortunately for Charles, the type of responsibility he will face as monarch in times of crisis was now being thrust upon him. At least Charles had his own 'rock' to lean on. Whatever the British public's feelings for Camilla Parker Bowles, it was to her he turned when coping not only with Diana's death, but the bureaucratic interference that seemed to be building behind it. For Charles, she was the voice of reason in a world that had been turned upside-down and it is, perhaps, a tribute to their love that he got through the ordeal.

As the week progressed, Charles and his sons found themselves settling into the routine that is familiar to so many who have suffered great loss. Practical matters had to be discussed, the details of the funeral for instance. William and Harry insisted they be allowed to walk behind their mother's coffin. Claims by some in Diana's camp that the Queen tried to veto this idea are simply not true. Her Majesty, in consultation with her husband, did ask Prince Charles if he felt the two-mile march in the muggy London heat might be a bit hard on the youngsters, but the final decision was left entirely to Prince Charles and his sons and, when they told the Queen they wanted to walk behind their mother's coffin, the Duke of Edinburgh immediately said he would join them.

During long afternoon walks on the Balmoral estate, Prince Charles spoke to his sons on all issues relating to Diana's death. He told them they were to take great comfort from the astonishing outpouring of grief that the world had shown on the occasion of their mother's death and he promised they would be able to see the staggering number of flowers and tributes that had been laid outside Kensington Palace back in London. The many books of condolence that had been signed in London, and the thousands of others that were due to pour into Buckingham Palace over the following months, would be kept in storage and made available to William and Harry whenever they wanted to read them.

Charles also told his sons they would hear and read about all sorts of ludicrous conspiracy theories that people who really should have known better were continuing to espouse. The prince, who had already been briefed extensively by both the Foreign Office and the Prime Minister, told them to ignore these stories; Mummy had died in a tragic, tragic accident and the only thing they would gain by believing the stories would be to diminish the guilt of those who were ultimately responsible.

It wasn't just that Fayed could not produce any hard evidence of an assassination; he couldn't produce any evidence. Harry was particularly concerned about Fayed's latest scheme, offering a million-dollar reward to anyone who could prove that Diana and Dodi were murdered. It is a measure of the utter lunacy of Fayed's theory that he honestly thought agent 006 was about to step forward and spill the beans.

There is no doubt that Britain's security services did keep a close eye on Diana after she had relinquished her police protection, but it was a routine operation, no different from the CIA monitoring close relatives of the President of the United States. Diana's decision to travel the world without any bodyguards was her own, but the decision to keep an eye on her was backed by the Queen, the Prime Minister and the police.

Almost a year after the crash, Fayed revealed the CIA, FBI and National Security Agency had more than a thousand pages of classified files on Diana. Considering the amount of spying these agencies are routinely involved in, and the fact they never talk to each other, it is not such a large file.

It is also absurd for Fayed to suggest Diana was murdered because the British public would never accept her marriage to Dodi, a Muslim. Firstly, Dodi was as devout a Muslim as Alex Ferguson is an Arsenal fan, and secondly, if that was the case why wasn't Hasnat Khan, Diana's real boyfriend and also a Muslim, taken out as well?

Diana herself was aware that the CIA was keeping an eye on her. She had already been told she would not be allowed to enter America without any form of protection. Quite simply, the United States Government did not want the responsibility of the world's most famous woman all alone in a country where gun violence claims more than 30,000 American lives a year. As D H Lawrence once wrote, 'the essential American soul is hard, isolate, stoic and a killer'. It wouldn't take much for a single nut to target the most famous woman in the world, and the CIA knew it. Once, when Princess Diana was on holiday in Martha's Vineyard, a row broke out between members of the press and the local police as Diana ate lunch in a small restaurant. The press had been told to clear off by two men who claimed to be security agents acting on the princess's orders. Diana was on holiday with her close pal, Lucia Flecha De Lima, the wife of the Brazilian Ambassador to the US. De Lima's personal protection officers were Brazilian and the press, mostly English, were complaining to local cops they had no jurisdiction over them. The matter was resolved when two men alighted from a car parked further up the street. The men, who had CIA written all over them, calmly informed the local police officer he would be facing a diplomatic incident if he allowed Brazilian bodyguards to tell American police officers to get rid of British journalists.

Both Prince Charles and the Queen had spoken at length to Britain's new Prime Minister, Tony Blair, since Diana's death. Mr Blair, who had been elected three months earlier with one of the biggest majorities in political history, had already shown an instant understanding of the nation's grief with his emotion-filled description of Diana as 'the People's Princess'. Now the man who was starting to come into his own in his new role of PM assured Charles and the Queen that whatever decisions were to be taken concerning Harry's and William's attendance at their mother's funeral were entirely a matter for the royal family. The gesture was appreciated; it was perhaps a relief for Charles and his mother to know that they wouldn't be bothered by the burden of political interference.

The Prime Minister was himself deeply affected by Diana's death. Having been told during the night of the tragedy, he had sat with his wife Cherie and discussed what to say at the hastily arranged press conference early that morning. Like most parents, their thoughts were with William and Harry. 'Oh those poor, poor children,' wept Mrs Blair. Her husband had been the first senior politician to take Diana seriously and had been determined to use her popularity for the benefit of the country. During a series of low-key lunches over the previous 12 months, Tony Blair, who at the time was Leader of the Opposition, had discussed with Diana the many options open to them in finding a job for her once Labour got back into power. Like the rest of the country, Diana had watched the Conservatives self-destruct under a sludge of sleaze and back-stabbing that made Watergate looked like a Sunday stroll in the park. It was no secret in Great Britain that a change of government was on the horizon as sure as a single European currency.

Diana saw herself concentrating on several major international issues, such as AIDS, famine and, of course, landmines, which she had taken an interest in only recently after seeing pictures from the Red Cross of mutilated children, blown up by the millions of unmarked mines still being planted throughout the world. But Tony Blair tactfully pointed out the political implications if Diana was to be involved in such controversial issues. Famine in Africa is so often caused by war as much as drought. Would Diana really want to put herself into a position where she might end up seriously criticising British or (God forbid) American foreign policy? And the issue of landmines was not as simple as people seemed to think. For the first time Diana would have to consider how she would react to serious criticism based on political and moral argument that would be thrown at her by intellectual heavyweights. How, for instance, would Diana react to the perfectly acceptable question, 'The damage inflicted by a landmine on a child's leg is nothing to the damage a nuclear bomb would cause ... what was Diana's stance on them?' There was also the issue of North and South Korea, two hostile relics of the cold war, divided by the world's biggest minefield. If all the landmines were lifted and the North invaded, this could lead to World War III. Would it really be worth standing among the nuclear radioactive wasteland that was once Great Britain saying, 'Well, at least they didn't throw any landmines at us'?

These questions, though extreme, were serious points the princess would have to face if she was going to be taken seriously on the international stage. Prime Minister Blair, following discussions with his own advisers, encouraged her to accept a far more ambassadorial role, allowing her to come under the protection of the Foreign Office and not be put on the spot by any number of points that would vex the most experienced politician.

Diana discussed all of this with both Harry and William. They both knew how keen she was to be guided by the young politician that most of the country was already recognising as Prime Minister in waiting, and were thrilled she had found a man with whom, as Margaret Thatcher said of Gorbachev, she could do business.

Diana followed Tony Blair's election campaign with the enthusiasm of the most ardent political watcher and spoke endlessly to her friends of the bright future she saw after a Labour victory. Her childlike excitement in all things political brought a smile to their faces. It was hard to believe the woman now heralding the arrival of a new Labour Government and earnestly discussing the rights and wrongs of a United Europe had once claimed to be 'as thick as a plank'. It was also no secret among Diana's tight circle of friends she had developed something of a crush on the young, good-looking Mr Blair, whose enigmatic smile still caused her to blush like a schoolgirl.

Unfortunately for Diana, the night of Tony Blair's victory

ended in disappointment for her. She had been in London driving with a male friend when the news came through at around 11pm that Tony Blair was the new Prime Minister. She immediately suggested they head to a Labour Party celebration ball she had an invitation to, but they were stopped by police in Park Lane. The police informed Diana the area was closed off due to what is euphemistically known as an 'incident'.

Rather than get caught up in the traffic, Diana headed back to Kensington Palace where she watched with glee as the Labour Party romped home with a massive majority. Diana also cheered when her old friend and mentor James Goldsmith launched into a tirade of abuse against defeated Tory candidate David Mellor. The multi-billionaire Goldsmith had long objected to Mellor's pro-Europe politics and now, as a candidate for the Independent Party, got the chance to watch the Tory MP's defeat and lecture the country on remaining British. Goldsmith was to die two months later from cancer at his home in Spain.

Following her tragic death, Prime Minister Blair, who did not get a chance to give Diana an ambassadorial role after all, gave her a title no political office or royal constitution can ever take away: the People's Princess.

Four days after Diana's death, the Queen decided the boys were coping well enough to be left at Balmoral with their father. Her Majesty would be travelling down to London where she was due to make her long-awaited television address to her people. Mounting press criticism had not been the reason she had decided to face the cameras. It was a gesture she had intended to make after the funeral but her advisers had pointed out the practicality of making the address now, when many people were still at a loss to know how to grieve Diana.

Looking the camera squarely in the eye, the Queen spoke as a 'Queen and a grandmother' and paid tribute to a woman who she described as 'an exceptional and gifted human being'. Her Majesty continued, 'In good times and bad, she never lost her capacity to smile and laugh, to inspire others with her warmth and kindness. I admired and respected her for her energy and commitment to others, especially for her devotion to her two boys.'

When a reigning monarch speaks, as the Queen did that day, to a global television audience with thousands of her subjects clearly visible in the background, it is hard to criticise or ignore her words. And it would be tantamount to treason not to believe them. The Queen's decision not to come down to London until the boys were ready had been vindicated. Not only had she been with William and Harry when they needed her most, she was now back with her people when, as the *Mirror* had pointed out, they had needed her most. As the nation turned off its TV it was clear that the grown-ups were back in charge.

On the eve of Diana's funeral her two sons were with her. Prince Charles had led William and Harry into the sombre Chapel Royal at St James's Palace where the coffin stood, draped in a flag symbolically bearing the royal coat of arms. Along with a rosary given to her by Mother Teresa and a photo of her father, Diana was to be buried with the two pictures of William and Harry that she had taken everywhere with her. The boys were offered the chance to see their mother a final time. William, with Prince Charles behind him, stepped forward. Prince Harry declined, keeping his eyes fixed on the back of his brother's neck as William whispered a final goodbye to the mother they had both adored. He then arranged a spray of white tulips at the head of the coffin. Only after it was sealed again did Harry step forward and place a wreath of white roses on the coffin. On top of this he left the white envelope with that devastating word 'Mummy' written on it.

The following day a third of the world's population watched television coverage of Princess Diana's funeral. It was a day drenched in sunshine. The crowd numbered tens of thousands, with many staking their claim for front-row views four days earlier and sleeping each night in the open air. An eerie silence filled the air, the only sound seemed to be the clip-clop of the horses as the coffin made its way down the London streets that Diana had known like the back of her hand. Harry and William made the trip to Westminster Abbey behind their mother's coffin without becoming emotionally overwhelmed, as the Queen had feared they might. The princes were flanked by Prince Charles, the Duke of Edinburgh and their uncle, Earl Spencer.

Harry followed the coffin with his arms stiffly at his sides. He was aware of the thousands of mourners who lined the route, but never once looked up. Like William, he was terrified of breaking down, even though his father had told both of them there was nothing in the world wrong with doing so.

Inside the magnificent Westminster Abbey, William and Harry stood side by side. Occasionally one of them would wipe away a tear; neither looked at the coffin. The most painful moment came right at the start of the service when Diana's favourite hymn, 'I vow to thee my country', was sung. Both being public schoolboys, Harry and William were as familiar with the words as their mother was and never failed to think of her when the hymn was sung at school. Now, with its so very British tune that conjured up images of royalty, empire and a thousand years of history, the hymn seemed unbearably poignant and the lyrics 'the dearest and the best' sadly apt.

When the time came for Earl Spencer to deliver his now famous eulogy, both Harry and William felt they were going to make it through. In some ways, the Earl's words, launching into a ferocious attack on the media and lobbing some thinly veiled criticism towards the royal family, came at exactly the right time. The contents of his speech, though deeply emotional when talking of Diana's virtues, allowed the boys' minds to wander away from the constant and immediate reminders of their mother's death. By castigating the media, Earl Spencer probably saved both boys from breaking down as each had approached the end of their emotional tether when Elton John had poignantly sang 'Goodbye England's Rose' only a few minutes before.

The tears flowed freely as Harry and William watched their mother's casket being lowered into the freshly dug grave on that sombre Saturday afternoon. The day, which had begun in glorious sunshine, was by now preparing to slip into dusk, and gathering dark clouds hinted at rain. Diana's body was laid to rest on a tiny island in the middle of the lake at Althorp, her family's home. As a child, Diana had often played on the island. Now, as the service ended and her two sons walked across a hastily erected pontoon bridge away from their mother's grave, they both knew she was finally home.

Two weeks later, on Monday, 15 September, it was Harry's 13th birthday. He had returned to school despite his father's offer for him to stay away for as long as he liked. The birthday was not one Harry felt any inclination to celebrate. Apart from anything else, the day he was to officially become a teenager had already been mocked by both Diana and William with warnings of impending manhood and having to grow up.

Unexpectedly, Harry had a visitor. It was his mother's sister, Lady Sarah McCorquodale, delivering the birthday present Diana had brought for him in Paris. Harry opened the package with his aunt in attendance. Inside was a Sony Playstation and a card that simply read:

Happy Birthday, Harry.
Love, Mummy.

CHAPTER EIGHTEEN

When he is not boarding at Eton, Harry lives with his father and Prince William at St James's Palace, the senior palace of the sovereign and still the 'court' to which foreign ambassadors and high commissioners are accredited. St James's, which Prince Charles moved into following his separation from Diana in 1992, was another home built by King Henry VIII, a king who would have made a good property developer. For over 300 years it was the official home of the reigning monarch until Queen Victoria moved to Buckingham Palace in 1837.

Harry and William have always had rooms at St James's but, following their mother's funeral, the two boys told their father they wanted all their personal effects moved from Kensington Palace to Charles's home. As the boys were staying at

Highgrove, and due to go back to boarding school, Charles said there was no great rush to move their personal belongings. Secretly Charles wanted to leave everything at Kensington Palace until the Christmas holidays when he figured the boys would welcome an excuse to go back to the home that was so full of joy whenever Diana was with them, but was too painful to return to just yet.

And Charles was right. During the Christmas week of 1997, ,when Harry had regaled everyone with his knockabout performance with the Spice Girls, he had been preparing himself for the visit to Kensington Palace he would be making with William the following day.

The visit turned out to be as difficult and emotional as Harry and William had expected, but at least it allowed them a final goodbye to the home they had once so loved. They were welcomed at the door by Diana's trusted servant, Paul Burrell. Both Harry and William had grown to love the man Diana once described as her 'rock' and now, as he took Harry's hand and led him up the familiar staircase, Burrell himself could not stop crying.

When the boys entered Diana's bedroom they were overcome with emotion. Like so many who return to the private quarters of a lost loved one, they half expected Diana herself to walk in at any moment and throw back her head in peals of laughter. Diana's favourite soft toys were arranged in their usual places, on her bed and chair. Harry and William helped themselves to several of the toys, as well as a number of photos in silver frames. They left behind a single photo of themselves with their mother. William retrieved a Cartier 'tank' watch that had been given to Diana by her father. He also took one special cuddly toy, a present from Prince Charles to Diana; it is a reminder of the time when his parents were in love.

Now that the boys had made their final visit to KP, the healing process could begin. Prince Charles encouraged them to talk about their mother, sometimes spending whole evenings with his sons as they spoke of the memories, often prompted by Charles himself, that brought huge smiles to their faces and the tears flowing again.

They also spoke of the continuing claims by Mohammed Fayed that Diana and Dodi were murdered, claims that grew more preposterous by the day. Following his initial assertion that the tragic car crash was no accident, Fayed now insisted it had been orchestrated by virtually every secret service in the world, including MI5 and the CIA. Nor did the stupidity stop there. Apparently, having failed to kill Diana in the car crash it now seemed they (the assassins) had access to the ambulance that took Diana to hospital and all the paramedics inside, forcing the vehicle to travel so slowly it would never make the ER in time to save her.

Had Fayed taken the time to research the security services before making his allegations, he would have learned that no agents would ever use a car accident as a means of assassination, as it is simply not effective enough. The impact of the crash killed Dodi and the driver instantly, but had Diana been wearing her seatbelt, like the bodyguard in front of her, she would be alive today. And the ambulance had to travel at a slow speed as the doctors inside were massaging

Diana's heart in an attempt to keep her alive. Fayed's allegations were an insult to the medical profession in France in general and the doctors and nurses who tried so desperately to save Diana in particular.

Charles told his sons to ignore this nonsense. They already had a deep loathing for Fayed following his attempts to convince the world that he had been informed of Diana's last words by a mysterious, unidentified lady at the hospital. Fayed claims that he was told Diana asked to be buried next to Dodi and that her sister Sarah was to take care of her children. It is hard to understand what makes a man come out with such nonsense. Fayed must know the hurt and confusion he is causing Harry and William. A woman severely injured in a car crash slipping in and out of consciousness does not suddenly make the decision to reverse every detail in her tightly packed will. Rather than living in cloud cuckoo land and making up fourth-rate movie script dialogue, Fayed should perhaps consider the damage he is doing to Diana's sons, family and friends when they are unexpectedly forced to listen to or read about this nonsense.

CHAPTER NINETEEN

As expected, Diana left the bulk of her estate to William and Harry. After various tax and death duties, the £24 million inheritance was whittled down to around £8 million each, which is kept in trust until the boys reach 25. With a trust fund already set up by his grandfather, Earl Spencer, Harry will be a very wealthy man in his own right one day.

Despite his wealth, Harry has never shown any signs of flaunting his money. He receives a substantial allowance from the Prince of Wales every four weeks but, as often as not, he still has most of the cash when another deposit is made the following month. Harry enjoys computer games and most of his spending ends up in his Playstation. He has a video and DVD in his room and is often seen at Our Price records in Peascod Street, Windsor, where he takes advantage of the three videos for £15 special offers. He also shops at the nearby Woolworths, as his mother did whenever she stayed at Windsor Castle, where he buys cut-price CDs and, on two occasions, girly posters for his den.

When Harry needs cash he wanders along Eton High Street to Coutts bank, situated across the street from a used-car showroom. After drawing his money, Harry often wanders across the road and looks in at the cars. At one stage, he was particularly impressed by an original Jaguar that had remained unsold for several months. On his next visit to Eton, Prince Charles was dragged down to the showroom where his expert advice on Jaguars was sought by Harry.

Harry prefers to walk the streets of Eton alone these days, and is often spotted deep in thought by local shopkeepers, who never point him out to their customers. Once, Harry was walking towards the fields at the back of Eton when he passed the public toilet, situated next to a small car-park on a four-shop parade. A young mother was standing outside the Gents with a child obviously in distress. Harry asked if anything was wrong, and the mother explained her six-year-old was desperate to use the toilet but felt he was too young to go in alone, and she couldn't really go in with him. Harry, as chivalrous as his elder brother, solved the problem by offering to stand outside the toilet while the mother went in with her son. Harry was prepared to stop others from using the toilet until she came out again. Admittedly, he did have a detective with him all the time, but it was still a spontaneous act of kindness of which his mother would have been proud.

After lessons have been completed on Saturday mornings, Harry likes to play football on the Eton pitches with several of his friends. They dress in an assorted choice of soccer clothes, Harry sporting either an Arsenal top or Eton one. He was once seen in a red England top he acquired just after his first England match against Colombia in 1998. Witnesses said it wasn't possible to see if it had BECKHAM on the back.

During the summer months Harry likes to play cricket in the same aggressive fashion he employs on the football field. The young prince is often out for a duck after stepping forward to smash a fast bowl far too early. Some of the old men, who seem to materialise with flasks and chairs whenever cricket is played at Eton, often point out Harry would be better off playing baseball.

Harry also loves cycling. Often he goes for a tough ten-mile ride that takes him as far north as Slough, and then back through Eton Wick and along the River Thames at Bovney Lock to Eton Bridge. He always stops on the bridge and looks down at the murky waters below. It is an amazing sight to watch the young prince, leaning slightly over the railing, the hundreds of tourists walking over the bridge oblivious to his presence. As he wanders off the bridge, walking his bicycle the final half mile to the college, Harry must reflect on his mother's claim that a normal life can be led as long as you don't draw attention to yourself.

Harry's favourite shop is a small general store at the top end of Eton High Street. After using the cash machine and looking in at the car showroom, he always makes his way to

Tudor Stores. The shop assistants greet him by name. Surprisingly for an English general store there are no newspapers inside, so Harry is spared the embarrassment of sensational newspaper headlines concerning his family.

Harry does not go out of his way to avoid the newspapers, though. The bookshop he has to pass on his way back to college has them prominently displayed out front. Often Harry will glance at a headline and then stop to read further, especially if it has front-page celebrity gossip concerning Jennifer Lopez, his favourite singer. Harry has a picture of the Bronx beauty with the infamous derrière on the wall of his den at Highgrove and has already told friends that Prince William is working out ways to contrive a meeting.

At night, Harry often rings Tiggy Legge-Bourke and the pair spend up to an hour idly gossiping. Long ago, Tiggy made Harry promise he would tell her if anything was ever wrong. Whenever they speak she asks him the same question and Harry always responds positively. Tiggy has told friends she always knows Harry's well when he answers the question with a laugh and a 'Yeah ... I'm OK.'

After talking to Tiggy, Harry will invariably compose a letter to his father. Prince Charles is well-versed in computer technology and receives e-mails from both his sons, but Harry knows he prefers the personal touch of a letter. If there is not enough time to read his sons' mail at breakfast, Prince Charles will place the letters in his briefcase and read them on his way to that day's official function. Harry learned the art of corresponding from his mother, who was a prolific letter writer, often composing thank-you letters and personal notes throughout the night with Harry by her side. When he writes to his father, Harry often decorates the letters with satirical cartoons on life at Eton. On one occasion, after his father had been promoted to Rear Admiral in the Royal Navy, Harry addressed his letter 'Rear Admiral Papa'.

When it is on air, Harry's favourite TV programme is *Big Brother*. Often criticised and dismissed as real-life TV for sad people who don't have a life of their own, the show has been a phenomenal success, regularly attracting 12 to 15 million viewers. Harry is particularly amused by the concept of taking eight ordinary people, throwing them into a house full of cameras and watching how they get on. He has told friends he would give anything to appear on the show. Although he knows this is not going to happen, Harry admits he is a *Big Brother* addict and even watches the internet version, broadcast 24 hours a day when the series is up and running. He also enjoys BBC costume dramas, often adaptations of books he has read. His particular favourite was *Pride and Prejudice*, which he watched on Tiggy's recommendation.

For many years Harry has acted out little plays and sketches with William and, just before the first anniversary of their mother's death, the boys decided to put on a play they had written for their father's 50th birthday party. Brazenly exploiting his royal privilege, William enlisted the help of Oscar-winning actress Emma Thompson to polish up the script. On hearing the news, actor Stephen Fry, a personal friend of Prince Charles's, demanded he be allowed to contribute. Between them they came up with a hilarious take-off of Prince Charles's 50 years, based on the popular

Blackadder format. Emma Thompson and Stephen Fry had cast themselves in several roles, before Rowan Atkinson agreed to come on board with one condition – that Harry and William join the much loved, multiple award-winning thespians on stage.

The single production took place at Highgrove on 31 July 1998. Though technically not even near Prince Charles' birthday, which was still three and a half months away, the date had been set due to the Prince of Wales's heavy workload and Harry and William's school commitments. The hundred or so guests at the bash, still being billed as Prince Charles' 50th birthday party, were charged £30 each for the privilege of being possibly the only people in history to see Harry and William appear on stage together.

The first anniversary of Diana's death was the most difficult for Harry. He had already decided, along with William, he wanted to be back at Balmoral when the day came. Both boys loved the vast country estate as much as their father did and looked forward to losing themselves on long walks across the acres of green, littered with the type of heather that shines in the sunlight.

On the actual date, 31 August, the boys attended nearby Crathie Church, as they had done on the day of her death, where they heard a service that included a reference to their mother. Despite polite requests for a statement from the press, the boys' only public gesture was to ask the Queen if all the flags in Britain could be flown at half mast. Her Majesty granted their request.

Strangely, members of the Spencer family were not

welcome at Crathie Church. Charles Spencer was beginning to pay the price for his thinly veiled attack on the royal family at Diana's funeral and his requests to be allowed to take part in the upbringing of Harry and William. What had angered Charles at the time of the speech was Earl Spencer's assumption that the boys would want to be with any family other than their own. An uncle has no claims on his nephews in any family if there is a remaining parent. It is also the natural inclination of families to drift apart following a death. In-laws are forced upon each other and rarely maintain any real contact once the bond that links them has gone.

Prime Minister Tony Blair attended the service. He arrived regally holding his wife Cherie's hand, appearing presidential and glamorous, his standard look these days. In no way did he resemble the sad, frustrated and tearful man who had faced the cameras on the day of Diana's death and spoke from the heart as no British Prime Minister has done since Churchill offered the country nothing but blood, sweat and tears.

The 22-minute service included a reading from the Twenty-third Psalm, which featured a line that brought great comfort to the young Prince Harry.

If I should walk in the valley of darkness
no evil would I fear.
You are there with your crook and your staff
with these you give me comfort.

Prince Charles has spoken at length with Harry about his
continuing relationship with Camilla Parker-Bowles. Both
his sons are aware of the love Charles and Camilla have
shared for many years, and see no reason why the couple
should not marry eventually. The boys refer to her as 'Papa's
friend' if she crops up in conversation. When they meet at
Highgrove, or St James's Palace, she is simply Camilla, and is
always greeted with a kiss on both cheeks by both boys.

Many times Charles has discussed the public's reaction to
Camilla with his sons. William, always more thoughtful when
it comes to big decisions, has told his father to continue
attending a series of low-key events with Camilla. William's
logic is that once the public gets used to them being 'an item'
it will be far easier to take the next step and announce a
formal engagement. Harry, in his usual manner, dismisses
any criticism of the relationship by the public and tells his
father, 'Who cares ... As long as you are happy.' Since his
mother's death, friends have noticed Harry increasingly
ignores potential problems with a shrug and a grin and the
words 'Who cares?' It is a reaction common in young people
who have undergone a traumatic experience.

Far too much water has passed under the bridge for either
William or Harry to be resentful of Camilla. Charles insists
to his children that no matter what happens in the future
with Camilla she will never replace their mother, nor would
he expect her to. Harry and William, aware that their father
is in his fifties, do not want to go out into the big wide world
and leave him alone in old age. When the time comes,
Camilla will take her place beside the only man she has ever

really loved and they will finally be the couple they should have been 30 years ago.